Telling the UN story

New approaches to teaching about the United Nations and its related agencies

Telling the
UN story

New approaches to teaching
about the
United Nations
and its related agencies

Leonard S. Kenworthy
Professor of Education
Brooklyn College
City University of New York

unesco - oceana

Published in 1963 by the United Nations
Educational, Scientific and Cultural Organization,
Place de Fontenoy, Paris-7ᵉ
and Oceana Publications Inc., Dobbs Ferry
New York
Printed by Vaillant-Carmanne, place Saint-Michel, 4, Liège

Foreword

As ever larger and more complex tasks are assigned to the United Nations and its related agencies by their Member States, these organizations are playing an increasingly important role in world affairs. But without widespread popular support, based on a knowledge and understanding of their aims, activities, limitations and possibilities, they cannot carry out their work with maximum effectiveness.

That is why the Member States of the United Nations, in resolutions adopted by the General Assembly, have urged that measures be taken to promote teaching about the United Nations and its related agencies. Resolutions to that effect have also been adopted by the Economic and Social Council of the United Nations and by the General Conference of Unesco. Considerable progress has been made in recent years in developing methods and programmes of education about the United Nations system, but much still remains to be done if people everywhere are to have an opportunity to learn about these organizations and their work.

This booklet is intended to encourage and assist teaching about the United Nations system in schools and other educational institutions and in out-of-school programmes for young people, adults or the community as a whole. The text was prepared, at the invitation of Unesco, by Leonard S. Kenworthy, Professor of Education at Brooklyn College, City University of New York.

Dr. Kenworthy, who was formerly a member of the Secretariat of the Preparatory Commission for Unesco and later of the Unesco Secretariat, is the author of many other books and articles on education for international understanding.

Some of the material for the booklet was drawn from the latest in a series of joint reports on teaching about the United Nations in Member States submitted in 1960 to the Economic and Social Council by the Secretary-General of the United Nations and the Director-General of Unesco. The author, however, was given complete freedom to express his own views, and comments therefore do not necessarily reflect the point of view of Unesco or of any other organization within the United Nations family.

It is hoped that the booklet will be a useful, practical aid to all those who are working to make the United Nations and its related agencies better known and understood.[1]

---

1. Publications on this subject issued earlier by Unesco, and now out of print, were: *Teaching about the United Nations and its Specialized Agencies: Some Recommendations and Suggestions*, Paris, Unesco, 1948 ; *Some Suggestions on Teaching about the United Nations and its Specialized Agencies*, Paris, Unesco, 1949 ; and *Teaching about the United Nations and its Specialized Agencies: A Selected Bibliography*, prepared by the United Nations and Unesco, Paris, Unesco, 1959. (Educational Studies and Documents No. 29.)

Contents

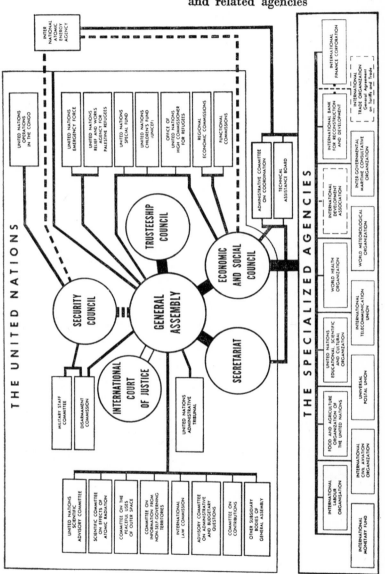

1　A new dimension in education

The citizens of all countries that are members of the United Nations and its related agencies should know about the United Nations organizations and should support the purposes of these intergovernmental bodies.

That is the gist of several resolutions passed by various bodies in the United Nations family since 1945. It is also the import of the two latest of these, one adopted by the Economic and Social Council on 6 April 1960,[1] and the other adopted by the General Assembly of the United Nations on 12 December 1960.[2] In the first, the official representatives of member governments re-affirmed their belief 'in the importance of teaching about the United Nations and its related agencies as a means of promoting interest in and support for their work'. In the second, they stated 'that knowledge and understanding of the aims and activities of the United Nations and its related agencies contribute to the fostering among young people of the ideas of peace and international co-operation and should therefore be promoted as widely as possible'.

Many people readily accept these resolutions and previous ones of a similar nature. Because their countries are members of the

1. Ecosoc res. 748(XXIX).
2. United Nations res. 1511(XV).

United Nations and have agreed to its purposes as a condition of membership, they recognize that their governments should foster teaching about the United Nations and its agencies both in schools and by other means. Some of them recognize such teaching as part of a new dimension to education everywhere—the international dimension. Others are more reluctant to accept the idea. They question the wisdom of the resolutions although they have been supported by the duly appointed representatives of their countries. They doubt the value of teaching about the United Nations or fear that it will diminish teaching for national loyalty. It is not surprising that some thinking people hesitate to support teaching about this new and enlarged international community of our day. It demands sharp readjustments in thinking and raises questions as to which institutions people should support.

Over the centuries men have often been confronted with similar questions. As new and larger groups of human beings were formed, smaller groups always had to decide whether they would add education for the wider community to their existing education. Despite difficulties, the new education has eventually been added by almost every smaller group. As a result of this general development, most people today are educated from early childhood to be effective citizens of their communities, often of larger political units within the nation, and of their nation. With the emergence of the international community we are now confronted with the question of the relation of education to this very large human unit. Consequently individuals, and a great many types of organization at the local, national and international levels, as well as governments, are seeking to solve the problem of the relation of education to this emerging community of the twentieth century. Should children, young people and adults be taught the facts about the emergence or existence of this community? Should they be educated to feel concern about its development? Should they be taught to support its intergovernmental institutions? Should they be educated to have a deep sense of loyalty to this global community? Questions like these are being asked all over the world today as parents, citizens, educators and government representatives try to determine the aims of education for life in an international community.

The governments that are members of Unesco have expressed their views on this broad and highly important question by asking the Unesco Secretariat to undertake a number of studies and pilot projects ranging from co-operation with national governments in the Associated Schools Project to a Major Project on Mutual Appreciation of Eastern and Western Cultural Values. The United Nations and Unesco have also examined the relevance of teaching about the United Nations and its agencies to education for life in the international community. The considered conclusion is that it is important for all citizens of their Member States to learn about the United Nations and its related agencies.

The first such resolution on this topic was passed as early as 17 November 1947.[1] It declared:

Considering that knowledge and understanding of the aims and activities of the United Nations are essential in promoting and assuring general interest and popular support of its work [the General Assembly of the United Nations] recommends to all member governments that they take measures at the earliest possible date to encourage the teaching of the United Nations Charter and the purposes and principles, structure, background, and activities of the United Nations in the schools and institutes of higher learning in their countries, with particular emphasis upon such instruction in elementary and secondary schools.

The wording of other resolutions over the years has varied only slightly from this text.

It is important to note that such statements are only recommendations to member governments. Nevertheless they have been voted by the official representatives of the members of the United Nations and/or Unesco and therefore reflect the thoughtful and considered judgement of national governments. It must also be pointed out that their aims are knowledge about, understanding of, interest in and support of the United Nations and its agencies. No recommendation has ever been passed implying blind allegiance to these international organizations or infringing the

---

1. United Nations res. 137(II).

sovereignty of Member States. All that has been proposed is that people be made aware of the significance of the United Nations and its agencies and that support of these international, inter-governmental organizations be sought. The assumption is that this would supplement rather than supplant teaching for national loyalty and complement rather than contradict education for nationhood.

Even to inform the people of the world of the purposes and programmes of the United Nations family of organizations seems a staggering assignment, but educators everywhere should work towards this with diligence and imagination. It is hoped that the suggestions in this small volume will stimulate educators in many parts ot the world to search for the most effective ways of teaching about the United Nations and its related agencies as a small but significant part of the larger and more difficult task of educating three thousand million people to live as neighbours in the rapidly emerging international community.

2 Aims and themes in teaching about the United Nations and its related agencies

Although it is very young the United Nations has grown into an organization encompassing a wide range of programmes. It is so vast and complex that government officials responsible for education, and educators in general, should consider carefully which aspects are to be stressed in schools, colleges and universities, and in adult education. It is also so new that the aims in teaching about it are not very clear. Nor is there general agreement as to what should be taught, where it should be studied, how it should be treated, or even why it should be included in curricula. Moreover, some of its work is controversial in nature and teachers are not always certain how such issues should be handled. Changes in the policies of national governments on some issues tend to complicate the work of the educator even more.

Perhaps it is significant that in all the reports of governments to Unesco and the United Nations on teaching about the United Nations and its related agencies[1] there have been very few references to the aims of such instruction. One reference in the 1960 report is found in an account of work in Sweden. This states that

1. Joint reports on teaching about the United Nations in Member States have been submitted to the Economic and Social Council by the Secretary-General of the United Nations and the Director-General of Unesco in 1950, 1952, 1956 and 1960. Fifty-four governments presented information for the 1960 report, which has been used in the preparation of this book.

In the teaching of history the teacher should strive for objectivity in presentation and caution in judgement, even in the description of international conflicts. The teacher should hold up to the pupils the importance of impartiality and humanity in opinions and judgements. His special aim should be to counteract the growth of hate and enmity against other peoples and races. The realization that mutual understanding and peace are essential to the progress of humanity should be encouraged in every way. Cultures and peoples should not be viewed in isolation, but their interdependence should be emphasized.

It would be useful if reports from Member States could include some clarification on the aims of teaching about the United Nations and its related agencies, which might stimulate thinking on this vital subject. If this is not feasible, governments and groups of educators might launch their own studies, with profit both to their own countries and to educators in other parts of the world.

Certainly clarity of aims is essential in any effective teaching. This is no less true with regard to teaching about the United Nations and its agencies than in relation to other themes. Once a teacher knows what he is trying to accomplish, it is much more likely that learning will take place. Conversely, if he is not sure of his aims, his students are not likely to be sure either. Once the aims are known, it is relatively easy to choose from a wide range of methods those most likely to bring about their achievement and the teacher can better select suitable materials or resources to use for the purpose. Finally, he can evaluate his teaching because the aims to appraise are clear.

This fourfold process of teaching and learning can be diagrammed in this manner:

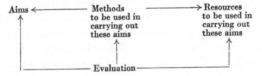

The task of suggesting broad outlines for any study in schools, colleges and universities, and adult education differs radically in the various Member States of the United Nations and Unesco. In most countries the general philosophy and aims for a particular subject are determined by the Ministry of Education or some similar overall body. In countries with a decentralized system of education, however, the task may devolve on smaller governmental units. Or there may be a combination of these two approaches. But even if the broad outlines, aims or themes are determined by a superior body much of the responsibility for translating these into action rests with individual teachers. In the final analysis it is they who carry out the aims whether they are decided by a superior agency or not. Appropriate bodies in every country should examine and clarify the general aims of teaching about the United Nations system and individual teachers should be instructed on them and/or encouraged to examine their meaning for themselves in relation to specific groups of children, young men and women, and adults.

There are seven general themes for teaching about the United Nations which the writer believes merit the attention of educators everywhere. They are discussed below.

Purposes of the United Nations

The Preamble to the Charter of the United Nations states the aims of the organization in simple and telling style. Briefly stated they are: (1) 'to save succeeding generations from the scourge of war'; (2) 'to reaffirm faith in fundamental human rights'; (3) 'to establish conditions under which justice and respect for the obligations arising from treaties and other sources of international law can be maintained', and (4) 'to promote social progress and better standards of life in larger freedom'.

This Preamble is a milestone in the history of man's efforts to create an international community based on freedom and justice. It is the Magna Charta of the world. It is important for it to be studied thoroughly, realistically and yet imaginatively. Its aims can be compared with those of other great charters of freedom and with the constitutions of various countries. Almost everyone agrees that these aims and the organizations which have been built to implement them represent a many-sided attack on war. There is widespread recognition that wars are not caused solely by political differences but by lack of social progress, the absence of human rights, economic inequalities and low standards of living. Thus the United Nations stresses, even more than the League of Nations did, the need for a socio-economic as well as a political approach to the creation and maintenance of a peaceful world.

The constitutions of the various agencies also merit study by persons interested in the United Nations, for they too state the aims of the United Nations, often listing in greater detail one or more of the four overall objectives mentioned in the Charter of the United Nations. For example, the Preamble to the Constitution of Unesco makes the bold and controversial statement that 'since wars begin in the minds of men, it is in the minds of men that the defences of peace must be constructed'. It avers that 'a peace based exclusively upon the political and economic arrangements of governments would not be a peace which could secure the unanimous, lasting and sincere support of the peoples of the world and that the peace must therefore be founded . . . upon the intellectual and moral solidarity of mankind'. It points out that 'ignorance of each other's ways and lives has been a common cause, throughout the history of mankind, of that suspicion and mistrust between the peoples of the world through which their differences have all too often broken into war' and suggests that 'the wide diffusion of culture, and the education of humanity for justice and liberty and peace are indispensable to the dignity of man and constitute a sacred duty which all nations must fulfil in a spirit of mutual assistance and concern'.

Any study of the United Nations and its agencies should include some attention to the reasons for their creation. This is true even of studies by children. The ideas they grasp may be very simple, but they should learn why the United Nations and its agencies exist.

One way is to help them see that countries have problems just as children and adults have and that they are trying to improve themselves and their relations just as human beings try to improve themselves and their relations. Another way is to encourage them to realize that wars cause a great deal of damage and that adults have organized a big international 'club' to try to prevent war and obtain peace. A third way is to point out that adults everywhere are anxious to make the world a better place for children to live in in the future. With older people it is, of course, much more complex. To the major aims, as stated in the Charter of the United Nations, will be added others ranging from the collection of pertinent information to provision of an international forum for the free expression of world opinion.

More mature students and some adults will want to examine the role of the United Nations and its related agencies in strengthening or creating a sense of world community. They could undertake the listing of the main factors moulding a community and then try to evaluate the United Nations in this light. Some of the factors that create a sense of community are a common past, shared values, a common language, common symbols, common law, common institutions, a common enemy or enemies, and a feeling of facing the future together. It should prove stimulating and helpful to see how many of these the United Nations provides.

Another purpose of the United Nations and its agencies is to serve as an expression of the highest ideals of people everywhere. In the Preamble of the Charter of the United Nations, the Universal Declaration of Human Rights, the Preamble of the Constitution of Unesco and other documents the dreams of men and women have been enunciated. There are echoes in them of the Declaration of Independence of the United States, the Bill of Rights of England, the French Declaration of the Rights of Man, Lincoln's Emancipation Proclamation, Sun Yat-sen's Principles of National Reconstruction and Gandhi's general philosophy. Many of the principles stated in these charters are far from being practised everywhere, but they are ideals towards which to strive. The United Nations as a moral force in the world is certainly another aspect to be stressed.

One of the briefest, yet most telling, descriptions of the reasons for the establishment of the United Nations is in the film, *World Without End*, in the statement that the United Nations was formed because people were 'ashamed of their past . . . and hopeful of their future'. Even more telegraphically the purpose of the United Nations and its agencies can be summarized in the phrase 'A better world'.

These are some of the ideas which should be emphasized in studies of the purposes of the United Nations.

Power of the United Nations

Another objective to be kept in mind in studies of the United Nations is an understanding of its power. One of the most common misconceptions is that it is a world government or body with power to act on a host of problems. This leads to much misunderstanding. People in many parts of the world ask, 'Why doesn't the United Nations do something about . . . ?', whatever problem or place they are worried about.

Students and adults have to realize that the United Nations has strictly limited power and that they must curb their expectations of it. It is an intergovernmental organization which cannot infringe on the sovereignty of nations. That is made very clear in the Charter where it is stated that 'Nothing in the present Charter shall authorize the United Nations to intervene in matters which are essentially within the jurisdiction of any State . . .'.

It should be remembered too that all the major powers approved the inclusion of the veto[1] power in the Security Council in the original plans for the United Nations, believing that little or nothing could be accomplished without the unanimous agreement of the Big Five.[2]

It is essential for understanding the United Nations that people realize its statements are really recommendations to sovereign States, except in a very few instances. However, it is equally important for people to know about the tremendous influence the

1. The 'veto' is the result of the voting formula laid down for the Security Council in Article 27 of the Charter. Decisions on procedural matters are made by an affirmative vote of any seven members; decisions on all other matters are made by an affirmative vote of seven members including the five permanent members, except that a party to a dispute shall abstain from voting on decisions relating to procedures for the peaceful settlement of the dispute. The 'veto' was jointly evolved by the Union of Soviet Socialist Republics, the United Kingdom and the United States of America before the San Francisco Conference, and reflected their conviction that the unanimous agreement of the Five Permanent Members of the Security Council was necessary for decisions affecting the maintenance of peace because of their major responsibility for it.
2. China, France, Union of Soviet Socialist Republics, the United Kingdom and the United States of America.

United Nations wields through the force of public opinion. Almost every government in the world now belongs to this international organization and those that are not members are eager to gain admission. One of the very first moves of most newly-independent countries has been to apply to join the United Nations. Moreover, no nation has withdrawn permanently, although a few have absented themselves temporarily from the General Assembly of the United Nations as a form of protest against action taken or about to be taken on a particular issue. Governments are very conscious of the power of world opinion and may even time statements made by their representatives in the United Nations so that they will be given the best possible coverage in the world's press, over the radio and on television in various parts of the world.

For some people studying the United Nations, it is important to include material on the shifts of power between its main organs. The best example is the decline in power and prestige of the Security Council and its gain by the General Assembly. This is due to several factors; amongst others the existence of the veto power in the Security Council and the desire of many small nations (including new members) to participate more fully in crucial decisions which they can in the General Assembly but not, usually, in the Security Council.

The 'Uniting for Peace' resolution of 3 November 1950[1] deserves attention from older students and adults as it gave the General Assembly much of its new power by enabling it to consider any threat to peace and security if the Security Council, because of lack of unanimity, was unable to act, provided that seven members of the Security Council or a majority of the members of the United Nations demand it.

Some groups will also want to examine the question of the extent to which the United Nations and its agencies have gained or lost power through the years. In his volume *United Nations and World Community*, the late Abraham H. Feller, the first Counsel of the United Nations, asserted that 'The Organization has shown little doubt or hesitancy that interpretation must be broadly conceived to foster the fullest possible utilization of its powers'.

1. United Nations res. 377(V).

There is considerable evidence to support his contention and the United Nations has grown in many ways since its formation. Its founders certainly were aware of the importance of economic and social affairs but it is doubtful if any of them foresaw the broad scope of the work the United Nations and its agencies now carry on through such organs as the Special Fund, the International Development Association or through Unesco's programme for educational assistance in Africa. Nor did they envisage the flexible role it would play in such political crises as those involving Suez, Lebanon and the Congo. Furthermore there are a number of fields in which the United Nations system is now working that were not contemplated by its founders, such as the peaceful uses of atomic energy, new sources of power and outer space. At the same time there is evidence that the United Nations has sometimes been by-passed by the Great Powers in their efforts to achieve solutions to thorny world problems. The pros and cons of such by-passing might well be examined by able students and adults.

*Programmes and progress of the
United Nations*

Many people know about the conflicts and controversies dealt with by the United Nations and its agencies. Such stories make exciting news. They are featured on the front pages of newspapers, in magazine articles and over the radio and television. Far too few people, however, know about the positive achievements of the United Nations system in hundreds of constructive projects all over the world. Lack of space permits the mention of only a few highlights of this remarkable story of progress. But these items, and scores of others not included, should be stressed in varying degrees with children, young people and adults in all programmes about the United Nations family.

In order to present a more comprehensive picture of the programmes and progress of the United Nations system, its accomplishments are grouped here under several general statements indicating the major areas in which the United Nations and its agencies are working. Among its many achievements are the following.

The United Nations system has done much to avert war and to settle disputes that were threats to peace and security. It is estimated that in the Second World War over 8 million men in the armed forces were killed and that civilian casualties ran into millions more. There were appalling losses in property and unbelievable suffering. Many parts of the world have still not recovered from this global holocaust. It was facts like these that led to the formation of the United Nations in 1945 with its resolve ' to save succeeding generations from the scourge of war, which twice in our lifetime has brought untold sorrow to mankind '.

Since its foundation the United Nations has had to concern itself with a succession of limited wars and threats of war. How well has it succeeded ? Opinions differ on this score but its accomplishments have been numerous. Here are the main disputes or conflicts dealt with by some part of the United Nations in its first fifteen years.

In 1946 Syria and Lebanon complained to the Security Council of the slowness with which British and French troops were being withdrawn from their countries. A resolution was passed favouring the speedy withdrawal of troops and these were quickly evacuated. Also in 1946 Iran objected to the Security Council about the delay in the Soviet troops' withdrawal from northern Iran and about political interference by the Soviet Union. The Security Council took up the case and adopted a resolution calling for an end to these troubles. The Soviet Union withdrew its troops peacefully. In 1946 again Greece brought an accusation against Albania, Bulgaria and Yugoslavia to the Security Council, charging that aid was being given to Greek rebel troops by these nations. The United Nations's Special Committee on the Balkans investigated the problem and eventually brought about a peaceful solution of the issues involved.

In 1947 fighting broke out between Indonesians and the Dutch. This dispute was brought to the attention of the United Nations by Australia and India and after more than two years of United Nations conciliation and mediation a peaceful settlement was achieved and the Republic of Indonesia was established as an independent sovereign State. In 1948 there was a bitter conflict over the establishment of Israel as a State. Although a peace treaty has never been signed, an armistice agreement was reached through the mediation of the United Nations. In 1948 India claimed that Pakistan was assisting tribesmen in an invasion into Jammu and Kashmir and sought the Security Council's aid in terminating the conflict there. A 'cease fire' agreement was arranged by the Security Council and a plebiscite in Kashmir promised. The plebiscite has not yet been held but the fighting has been stopped and an uneasy peace restored.

In 1950 the Security Council took action to assist the Republic of Korea by sending troops there in a collective military action. After months of negotiation, a truce was signed on 27 July 1953 and an extensive programme of relief and rehabilitation begun. However, the United Nations is still seeking peaceful unification of Korea, at present divided into two countries. In 1956 the United Nations General Assembly called on the U.S.S.R. to stop armed attacks against Hungarians and to withdraw Soviet troops from that area. This measure was not recognized by the U.S.S.R. as valid and it took no action to comply with it. Also in 1956 the United Nations General Assembly called on Britain, France, Israel, and Egypt to halt hostilities and the troops of Britain, France and Israel were asked to withdraw from Egypt. A United Nations police force was sent in to supervise a truce and a United Nations mission was sent to reopen the Suez Canal which had been blocked.

In 1960 the Congo was granted independence by Belgium and an internal struggle immediately ensued. Help was requested from the United Nations and troops were dispatched. A complicated struggle continued within the new nation despite United Nations interventions. As this book is being written comparative calm has settled over the Congo but the permanent settlement of the troubles there is not yet in sight.

These disputes are some of the highlights of recent history but there are many others not included in this brief résumé.[1] Yet in spite of the risk of war in several situations, global conflict has been averted. Other disputes have been aired in the General Assembly, which has often acted as a 'safety valve'. Sometimes

1. Detailed accounts of these and other questions are given in *Everyman's United Nations* published by the United Nations.

it has been possible for diplomats to iron out difficulties through personal contacts—in the Delegates' Lounge at the United Nations, at social functions and at private gatherings.

In these and other ways the United Nations has been alert to prevent war and settle disputes which might lead to war. This is a creditable record for a new organization with strictly limited powers.

The United Nations system has done much to assist refugees. Wars and revolutions from time immemorial have caused displacements of people, but the number affected has never been as large as in this century. While not all refugees have been the subjects of international action, three United Nations agencies have been concerned with particular groups: The United Nations High Commissioner for Refugees (UNHCR); the United Nations Relief and Works Agency for Palestine Refugees (UNRWA); and the United Nations Korean Reconstruction Agency (UNKRA).

International assistance to refugees was first organized in 1921, with the appointment of the League of Nations High Commissioner for Refugees, and continued in some form until the beginning of the Second World War. After the war, the United Nations Relief and Rehabilitation Administration (UNRRA) undertook the relief, repatriation and resettlement of displaced persons and refugees. Later the International Refugee Organization (IRO) continued these operations.

UNHCR, which came into being in January 1951, provides international protection to the 1,300,000 refugees within its mandate and seeks permanent solutions to their problems by facilitating their voluntary repatriation or their assimilation into new national communities. To date, 60,000 refugees have been firmly settled by UNHCR and 50,000 others helped toward resettlement at a cost of $40 million to UNHCR and $50 million to the asylum countries. Thousands more were resettled without cost to the organization, thanks to its overseas resettlement schemes.

UNHCR also deals with new refugee problems; for example, it provided maintenance and shelter to over 200,000 Algerian refugees in Morocco and Tunisia and also assisted in the orderly return of these refugees to their homes at the cessation of hostilities.

Both operations were carried out jointly with the League of Red Cross Societies.

Under its 'good offices' function, UNHCR has been asked to assist Chinese refugees in Hong Kong and Macao, refugees in Cambodia, refugees from Tibet, refugees from Angola in the Congo, refugees in Togo, refugees from Ruanda in the Congo, Burundi, Tanganyika and Uganda, and Cuban refugees in Spain.

An equally heavy assignment was handed to UNRWA as a result of hostilities over the creation of the State of Israel. Over a million refugees, about half of them under 17 years of age, are registered with UNRWA. The agency operates in Jordan, the Gaza Strip, Lebanon and the Syrian Arab Republic, and its relief programme provides food, shelter and medical care. Of prime importance is UNRWA's education and training programme which provides basic education for refugee children and vocational training for many young people. In its work UNRWA has the help of other parts of the United Nations system, such as the World Health Organization (WHO) and the United Nations Educational, Scientific and Cultural Organization (Unesco).

The third agency created to deal with refugees was the United Nations Korean Reconstruction Agency which aided nearly 700,000 refugees to build new homes or to repair war-damaged ones and assisted many others by the extension of relief. Its work was terminated on 30 June 1958.

The United Nations system has done much to liquidate colonialism and to foster new independent nations. In the eighteen years since the signing of the United Nations Charter at San Francisco the number of dependent peoples in the world has fallen by about 800 millions. In that time more than thirty formerly dependent territories have attained independence. In 1960 no fewer than eighteen newly independent nations, seventeen of them in Africa, emerged from dependent status of one form or another. Several other non-self-governing lands are on the threshold of nationhood and by the end of 1962 the United Nations 'family' of Member States had grown from eighty-two (in 1958) to one hundred and ten.

The United Nations has an important role in the evolution of dependent peoples towards self-government and independence.

Written into Chapter XI of the Charter is a declaration of principles regarding non-self-governing territories that recognizes them as a 'sacred trust' and provides that the countries administering these territories are accountable to the world community for the peaceful progress of their inhabitants. Chapter XII of the Charter provides for actual United Nations supervision over a small number of territories which have been placed under the international trusteeship system by separate agreements between the administering authorities and the United Nations. The United Nations Trusteeship Council, under the authority of the General Assembly, has the task of supervising the administration of the Trust Territories, of furthering their economic and social advancement and of helping their peoples to move towards self-government or independence.

By the end of 1962, eight of the territories under trusteeship had become independent countries, or a part of an independent nation. These were: the French Cameroons and Togoland, now the Republic of Cameroon and Togo; the British Cameroons, the northern section of which has become a part of Nigeria and the southern section a part of the Republic of Cameroon; British Togoland, which has become a part of Ghana; Somaliland, which becomes the Republic of Somalia; Tanganyika, the largest territory formerly under trusteeship; Western Samoa; and Ruanda-Urundi, which becomes the two independent States of Rwanda and Burundi. Thus a majority of the eleven trust territories of the United Nations have gained political freedom in the eighteen years of United Nations history, an achievement that is in line with the purpose of the trusteeship system.

To speed the progress of the peoples of all remaining dependent territories,[1] both trust and non-self-governing, the United Nations General Assembly on 14 December 1960 took one of its most far-reaching measures on colonialism by adopting a *Declaration on the Granting of Independence to Colonial Countries and Peoples* [2] that '*solemnly proclaims* the necessity of bringing to a speedy and unconditional end colonialism in all its forms and manifestations'. Chandra S. Jha of India, chairman of the Special Committee of

1. Four of the eleven trust territories had already gained their independence.
2. United Nations res. 1514(XV).

Seventeen established subsequently to study and promote the application of the declaration, described the adoption of this statement as 'truly one of the landmarks in the history of the United Nations'.

The United Nations system has done much to promote economic and social progress and better standards of living. Most of the people of the world today are ill-fed, ill-clothed, ill-housed, illiterate and ill. They eke out a meagre existence by scratching the soil with sticks or wooden ploughs or by fishing in lakes and streams and rivers. They do not have enough of the right kinds of food to maintain health. They resort to superstitious practices to cure disease or do without medical help, and great numbers die at an early age. Schools do not exist in their communities or they are new and access to them is limited. For centuries such conditions have existed in large parts of the world. People accepted their lot as inevitable. But today there is a revolution of rising expectations everywhere. People know that life can be better and they are determined to share in the good things of this earth.

In this world-wide revolution against poverty, disease, ignorance and prejudice the United Nations and its agencies are taking an active part. In almost any part of the world at this moment a United Nations representative or team of experts is at work showing people how to turn deserts into fertile regions, how to conquer malaria and yaws, how to build bridges and highways, how to improve the water in the village well or how to 'plant' fish in the village pond in order to improve the protein diet of the villagers, how to dredge a port or build an airport, how to build a school or become a teacher, how to start a health clinic in a small town or a community centre in a rapidly growing metropolitan area.

Much of this work is carried on by the specialized agencies of the United Nations under their own programme and with their own funds. But much of it is also administered by the agencies with funds from the Expanded Programme of Technical Assistance. Since its establishment in 1950 this programme has financed the work of nearly 15,000 experts from more than one hundred countries in field assignments in 140 nations and territories. In addition it has awarded nearly 18,000 fellowships to men and women for advanced study in other countries so that they could acquire more knowledge and other skills with which to work in their home lands.

To give even greater emphasis to this task, the United Nations General Assembly, by unanimous vote in December 1961, designated the 1960s as the United Nations Development Decade.[1] It called upon all member nations for a sustained effort to break the cycle of poverty, hunger and disease and to achieve for the 'depressed' two-thirds of the world new levels of economic and social well-being. The resolution sets a definite goal of a minimum annual rate of growth of national income of 5 per cent, to be achieved in the less-developed countries before 1970. It points out that economic and social progress are not only of primary importance to these countries, but also basic to the attainment of international peace and security, and to a faster increase in world prosperity.

The enemy that the Food and Agriculture Organization is fighting is hunger. Its officials estimate that two-thirds of the world's people suffer from serious undernourishment and that not more than one family in a hundred ever has a good nutritious meal. To complicate their task there are 140,000 more people in the world each day. By the year 2000 the world population is expected to be around 5,000 million or nearly double the present figure. But much can be done by the collection of pertinent statistics, research in laboratories and in the field, conferences where 'know-how' is exchanged, advising governments on their problems and by demonstration projects; and FAO has proof of the results that can be obtained. The poultry production of Cambodia was increased 50 per cent by an improvement scheme inaugurated in 1957. The introduction of an improved variety of rice in Egypt has increased rice production by 180 per cent. Until a few years ago El Salvador had to rely on imported dairy products. Today it has 200,000 dairy cows for a population of only 2.3 million and

---

1. See *The United Nations Development Decade: Proposals for Action*. New York, United Nations, 1962, 125 p. $1.25, 8/6 (stg.), 5 Sw.Fr. (United Nations sales No. 62.II.B.2).

is no longer dependent on imports of dairy products. These are only three of the scores of projects of this specialized agency, which has achieved astonishing results in a short period of time.

The enemy the World Health Organization is fighting is disease. Its funds are severely limited and its staff small so it has to produce the maximum in results with the minimum in outlay. It therefore concentrates on the training of doctors and public health officials, the establishment of schools to train health personnel, the development of new vaccines and their production in many parts of the world, service to the medical profession throughout the world by acting as a clearing house of information and campaigns against a limited number of diseases. In 1959 WHO was able to report that 'malaria eradication is now a global programme'. The population in areas freed of malaria totalled 305 million by 1962. Eradication programmes in operation at present cover 767 million more people. The advantage of eradication: land long infested with malaria is now available for cultivation and farmers once too weak to work are able to plant and harvest. In leprosy campaigns nearly 2 million patients were under treatment in 1962 and the effectiveness of new drugs and home treatment, without old methods of segregation, has been proved. In the fight against yaws, a crippling disabling disease, the rate of infection has been reduced in some areas from 20 per cent or more of the total population to less than one-tenth of 1 per cent.

The enemies that the United Nations Educational, Scientific and Cultural Organization (Unesco) contends with are illiteracy, ignorance and prejudice. It is estimated, for example, that 700 million persons can neither read nor write in any language and that almost half of the world's children never go to school. Prejudice knows no national frontiers; it is an international problem. It exists everywhere—in different forms. So does ignorance. Yet the task of Unesco is to promote peace and security through education, science and culture on a budget of approximately $37 million per year (including around $18 million from the Expanded Programme of Technical Assistance of the United Nations, the Special Fund and other sources) which must be used for more than one hundred nations.

How can this be done? First, Unesco can assemble useful

information and disseminate it throughout the world. Then it can give scholarships for travel and study abroad to key educators, scientists and cultural leaders to increase their knowledge and experience so that they may perform their jobs better in their home countries. Next it can call conferences in which experts in various fields share information and take new ideas back home to put into practice in large areas. Further it can publish useful materials in several languages and thus reach many millions of people. Often it works with Unesco National Commissions and Co-operating Bodies in each of the Member States so that its work can be increased many times. It also carries on leadership training programmes by establishing such centres as those at Patzcuaro, Mexico and Sirs-el-Layyan, Egypt, where potential leaders of adult education programmes are trained. There are scores of projects which Unesco carries on, but in recent years it has concentrated on four—the extension of adult education in many parts of the world; aid to the nations in the arid zone that runs from North Africa through the Middle East to South Asia for improvement of their land; the extension of free and compulsory primary education, and assistance to all Member States in further-ing mutual appreciation of Eastern and Western cultural values.

Each of the thirteen specialized agencies, the four regional economic commissions, the Special Fund and other parts of the United Nations family, work in similar ways to promote the eco-nomic and social well-being of the people in the Member States of the United Nations and its agencies. The three agencies men-tioned above were selected because their efforts are probably most readily understood by children. The work of Unicef (United Nations Children's Fund) will be treated briefly in the next section of this chapter as it, too, is readily understood by the young.

The United Nations system has done much for women and children. The work of all parts of the United Nations system affects women and children but there are two members of the United Nations family especially concerned with them. They are the Commission on the Status of Women and Unicef.

Equal rights for women is a relatively recent development for a good many nations and a status which has not been reached in many countries. As part of its pledge in the Charter 'to reaffirm fundamental human rights' the United Nations in 1946 established a Commission on the Status of Women. This body prepared a Convention on the Political Rights of Women which the General Assembly adopted in 1952 and that has now been ratified or acceded to by thirty-seven nations. These countries admit the right of women to vote, hold public office, serve on juries and take part in public institutions. The Commission has urged the United Nations Visiting Missions to Trust Territories to inspect the rights of women and to promote better conditions for them in those areas. It has also studied other inequalities such as differences in public service opportunities for women and men and unequal pay for women who perform the same jobs as men. Even more important, it has studied the problem of equal rights for women in education. Its results to date have not been startling but it has made progress and alerted many nations to tasks which should be undertaken.

The hundreds of millions of needy children in the world are the primary concern of Unicef. The agency's name has become a household term for millions of families, particularly in the developing countries, and has therefore been retained as the hallmark of this organization despite the fact that its official title is now the United Nations Children's Fund (omitting the words 'international' and 'emergency' which were included in its original title).

Since its creation in 1946, Unicef, working closely with the WHO and the FAO, has participated in testing about 400 million young people for tuberculosis and in vaccinating over 150 million against the disease. It has assisted in the treatment of more than 30 million people for yaws, effecting a cure in many instances with a few cents worth of penicillin. It has aided projects that have treated over 9 million children afflicted with trachoma, the dreaded eye disease found in the geographical belt from Morocco to Taiwan. It has helped malaria eradication campaigns in sixty countries, leprosy control in thirty-four; and for years it has been providing over 5 million daily rations of milk to undernourished children and mothers.

But Unicef's efforts go far beyond such important help as this.

It is concerned also with such lasting improvements as the establishment of maternal and child health centres, local production of safe milk or other high-protein foods, nutrition education, and the training of midwives, public health nurses and other national personnel. Recently Unicef extended its scope beyond health and nutrition to include aid to broad social services, education, vocational training and other projects recipient countries consider of high importance for their children. It will even help countries establish their priorities and plan comprehensive action programmes. These new types of aid will bring Unicef into close relationship with Unesco, the International Labour Organisation and other appropriate United Nations agencies.

Though an integral part of the United Nations (it is not a specialized agency) Unicef is financed by voluntary contributions from governments and individuals. Governments of countries in which it works administer the Unicef-aided projects and are expected to match the imported supplies or other aid with buildings, staff and locally available supplies.

Through many dramatic and some not so dramatic activities, this member of the United Nations family is attempting daily to implement the statement in the United Nations Declaration of the Rights of the Child that 'Mankind owes to the child the best it has to give'.

The United Nations system has done much to state the hopes and aspirations of mankind. Any community needs some commonly shared values to have a modicum of unity among its members. This is as true of the international community as of other units of society. In the Preamble of the Charter of the United Nations, the Universal Declaration of Human Rights and the Declaration of the Rights of the Child member governments of the United Nations have set forth some of these shared values. These are statements of ideals, declarations of intent. That they are not generally implemented at present is readily agreed. However, men need to be pulled forward by their ideals as well as driven by their basic needs. Thus the rights asserted in these various charters are goals toward which mankind should work and in many cases is now working.

The statement of such aims is another of the varied services of the United Nations family, quite different from its programmes of action but equally important. Work is proceeding on two draft International Covenants on Human Rights to formulate in greater detail the aspirations outlined in the United Nations Charter. One of them deals with civil and political rights, the other with economic, social and cultural rights.

Conclusion. The United Nations system, as an instrument to establish peace and security, promote human rights, establish conditions under which justice can be maintained and promote social progress and better standards of living in greater freedom, has, in eighteen years, accomplished a great deal, as the examples in this section show. Many more could be given.

People of the United Nations

The United Nations is primarily an organization. But it is also people. It is important to bear this in mind when considering the aims of teaching about the United Nations and its agencies, especially with young people who tend to be more interested in stories of men and women than younger boys and girls. The possibilities in developing this theme are numerous. Many will want to include in any study of the United Nations stories of the statesmen who helped to found it and the part each played in the creation of the United Nations system. Accounts could be given of the three Secretaries-General, Trygve Lie, Dag Hammarskjöld and U Thant, and also, perhaps, some of these men's chief lieutenants in the Secretariat. This would be especially appropriate in countries from which men in these high posts have come.

Another commendable practice is to include brief profiles of the various presidents of the General Assembly. Since they have come from so many different nations a study of them helps people to see the international structure of the organization. Starting from the beginning, the presidents have been as follows: 1946—Paul-Henri Spaak of Belgium; 1947—Oswaldo Aranaha of Brazil; 1948—Herbert Evatt of Australia; 1949—Carlos Romulo of the Philippines; 1950—Nasrollah Entezam of Iran; 1951—Luis

Padilla Nervo of Mexico; 1952—Lester B. Pearson of Canada; 1953—Mrs. Vijaya Lakshmi Pandit of India; 1954—Celco N. van Kleffens of the Netherlands; 1955—José Maza of Chile; 1956—Prince Wan of Thailand; 1957—Sir Leslie Munro of New Zealand; 1958—Charles H. Malik of Lebanon; 1959—Victor Belaunde of Peru; 1960—Frederick H. Boland of Ireland; 1961—Mongi Slim of Tunisia; 1962—Muhammed Zafrulla Khan of Pakistan.

Much can be gained from a study of the lives of the heads of the specialized agencies. Through the lives of these men, children and young people can obtain a lot of useful information about the United Nations and its accomplishments. It is also important to include some study of the role which women have had in the United Nations family of organizations. Typical of those who could be studied are the late Gabriela Mistral, the noted Chilean poet, educator and Nobel Prize winner, Mrs. Franklin D. Roosevelt of the United States and Mrs. Vijaya Lakshmi Pandit of India. Lesser known people, too, have a place in such studies. These might include members of the United Nations Secretariat in New York City or men and women carrying on technical assistance programmes in many parts of the world.

Then again, students should be helped to realize that the United Nations also includes the countless inconspicuous individuals affected by it: the peasant who has just received a plough with a metal tip so that he can produce crops more easily and better; the child who has been inoculated against yaws and whose health is now greatly improved; the families of a village where the protein diet has been increased by the 'planting' of fish in the community pond; the tradesman who can carry more produce to market because of improved roads in his district; the international traveller whose safety and health is protected by the work of the International Civil Aviation Organization and the ordinary citizens everywhere whose lives are being saved by efforts to prevent global warfare.

Such studies of the United Nations through the personalities of those carrying out the work of the organization and those affected by it, can be an exciting and worthwhile approach to the organization and its related agencies.

Problems of the United Nations

Studies of the United Nations and its agencies for upper primary grade children should pay some attention to the problems of the organizations while those for secondary school and college students should devote a great deal of time to them. For adults the difficulties involved in making the United Nations and its agencies strong and effective should also be presented.

Teachers should be realistic in teaching about the world and this includes facing the problems which beset the United Nations family. Perspective on these is gained if students are made aware of the difficulties involved in families, communities and nations. They may then ask themselves how much more difficult it is to evolve the proper structure for an international organization including over a hundred nations, and to reach decisions which can be supported by these countries of such divergent interests and needs. One approach is for students to become acquainted with those problems with which the United Nations must wrestle, such as disarmament, the control of atomic energy, colonialism, discrimination and prejudice, low standards of living, education, the training of governmental officials and the raising of capital for industrialization. Mention has been made in the foregoing section of a few of the efforts of the United Nations and its agencies to cope with these.

There are other problems besetting the world with which the United Nations deals only indirectly such as the basic need for land reform within nations and the tensions which, arising within countries, may yet have international repercussions. There are the unsettled disputes which have accumulated during the eighteen years of the United Nations' existence such as the difficulties over Kashmir, Korea and the Congo.

In the solution of many of these problems there is the paralysing influence of the ideological struggle between the two great blocs. As Dag Hammarskjöld, the late Secretary-General of the United Nations, phrased it in his annual report to the United Nations in 1960: 'With its constitution and structure, it is extremely difficult for the United Nations to exercise an influence on problems which are clearly and definitely within the orbit of present-day conflicts between the power blocs.' This in turn leads to the problem of by-passing the United Nations in the search for solutions to some of the major issues of the day.

Another difficulty arising from the United Nations' lack of power is the question of what measures it can take when nations feel that problems under discussion are clearly issues of an internal nature. A case in point is the problem of South-West Africa which the Republic of South Africa maintains is an internal affair; another is that of Portuguese Angola. Still another difficulty is how to strengthen the authority of some of the existing organs such as the International Court of Justice. There is also the question of whether a permanent police force or a permanent peace force should be organized by the United Nations, replacing the United Nations Emergency Force which has been used in such situations as the Suez and Congo crises.

Added to these world-wide problems are a number of issues which concern the purposes and structure of the United Nations itself. For example, there is a strong feeling on the part of many members of the United Nations that the nations of Asia and Africa are not adequately represented in the Security Council or the Economic and Social Council. Membership of these bodies was determined before the admission of the many new nations which have joined the United Nations in recent years, and these assert that they should be far better represented in these key organizations than they are at present. The question of the admission of the People's Republic of China is another highly important and extremely controversial issue.

In 1960 the Soviet Union presented a plan for a tripartite directorate for the United Nations in which the two opposing power blocs and the neutral or uncommitted nations would be equally represented. This is a radical departure from the existing executive agreement and calls for a major decision which must be made in the months ahead.

The question of the size of the United Nations has also been posed by some nations. The facilities of the United Nations headquarters in New York are already inadequate and changes will certainly have to be made in the physical arrangements, if not also in other aspects, of the organization. There is likewise some criticism of the voting procedure of the United Nations whereby nations with large populations have the same vote on all measures as nations with very small ones. Various plans have been presented for 'weighted voting', according to population or wealth but so far there has been no unanimity on the need for change. People have also criticized what they term 'diplomacy by radio and television'. These critics maintain that more harm than good is done to the organization by the public broadcasting and telecasting of its proceedings, but up till now pressure for change in this regard has not been great.

These are some of the problems of the United Nations family today with which students should be familiar and that more mature persons should analyse. Critical and clear thinking on them is certainly a part of good education anywhere and an understanding of these and other problems should lead to a better understanding of the United Nations system.

Perspective on the United Nations

Still another aim in studying the United Nations and its related agencies should be to see these organizations in historical perspective. Since children have little sense of time, this theme should be limited to more mature students and adults. The United Nations should be seen as the latest and most ambitious of man's attempts to break down the barriers separating people and nations and create a peaceful and just international community. The beginnings of such efforts go far back in history. They present a long and almost unending series of plans outlined by the pioneers of world peace.

Just where one starts in such a study is problematical. Perhaps a start could be made with Pierre Dubois (1307) and his *Plan for the Peace of Europe* to end the Crusades and provide a permanent Court of Arbitration to avert conflicts. In 1309 Dante proposed in his book *The Kingdom* that all nations live under one law. In 1517 the Dutch scholar Erasmus wrote *The Complaint of Peace* in which he proposed a Council of Just Men to deal with international disputes 'so that wars shall not breed wars'. In 1595 the French statesman, Sully, presented his Grand Design with its suggestion of a Council of Europe to prevent any one nation from gaining the hegemony of that part of the world. As part of this plan he called for an armed force based on the quota system. In 1623 Emeric Crucé of France went even further, including India and China in his plan for a World League. Realizing that economic motives caused war as much as political differences he called for attention to this aspect of the problem. He proposed a permanent council located in a neutral city and a 'universal police' if plans to avert trouble broke down. In 1625 the Dutch lawyer Hugo Grotius developed the idea that laws should apply to nations as they did to individuals. He is considered by many to be the father of international law.

In 1693, William Penn proposed a European federation in a little book called *An Essay Towards the Present and Future Peace of Europe*. This plan included the Turks and the Muscovites as well as representatives of Western and Central Europe. He even suggested the use of Latin and French as the two international languages to be used by the delegates to a European Parliament. *A Project for Perpetual Peace* was the title of the Abbé de Saint-Pierre's plan, published in Paris in 1716, in which he proposed a Union of Monarchs. His suggestions included a President of a Senate, to be called the 'Prince of Peace', judges and an armed force. In 1761 Jean-Jacques Rousseau worked out a very similar plan, known as *A Lasting Peace*. Immanuel Kant of Germany drafted a detailed plan in 1795 for a federation of free States which he called *Toward Perpetual Peace*. In it he proposed the abolition of national armies and the creation of an international police force as well as the establishment of a common law for all nations.

These were some of the early plans for peace. They have been described in some detail as they are not always included in the historical background of the United Nations. From that time on the story is better known to students. It includes the Congress of Vienna, with occasional meetings of the major powers thereafter as part of the Concert of Europe which lasted intermittently up to the First World War. It also includes the establishment of the Universal Postal Union in 1874 which has continued to the present time and is now a specialized agency of the United Nations. Mention should be made too, of the Hague Conference of 1899 where both large and small nations met on an equal basis to discuss ways of keeping the peace. The conference set up the Permanent Court of Arbitration, a forerunner of the present International Court of Justice.

In any study of the United Nations and its related agencies some attention should be paid to the League of Nations, with special reference to the causes of its decline. The League went far beyond any previous attempt at international organization. It dealt with a wide range of social, economic and cultural matters as well as with problems of collective security. Study of the League will throw a great deal of light on the formation of the United Nations and especially of the Economic and Social Council and the specialized agencies.

In the booklet he prepared for the United Kingdom's National Commission for Unesco, C. F. Strong telescopes this long history in these words:

It is, of course, true to say that the plan of the United Nations is the latest of a long line of projects of political internationalism, from the paper schemes of Pierre Dubois, Erasmus, Henry of Navarre, the Abbé de Saint-Pierre, Rousseau and Kant, through the Congress system and the Concert of Europe, whose tinkling music was finally played out by the discordant trumpets of Bismarck's Machtpolitik, to the Hague Conferences and the League of Nations.[1]

From the outbreak of the First World War until the formation of the United Nations in San Francisco on 24 October 1945, different people will select different dates for an abbreviated history of the United Nations. But most will agree that these dates are important: 14 August 1941, the promulgation of the Atlantic Charter; May 1943, the Conference on Food and Agriculture when the Food and Agriculture Organization was formed; October 1943, the Moscow Declaration by China, Great Britain, the U.S.S.R. and the U.S.A. recognizing the necessity of an international organization; August 1944, the Bretton Woods Conference at

1. C. F. Strong, *Teaching for International Understanding: An Examination of Methods and Materials*, London, Her Majesty's Stationery Office, 1952, 96 p.

which the International Bank and Monetary Fund were established; February 1945, the planning of the San Francisco Conference by Churchill, Roosevelt and Stalin; and April 1945, the San Francisco Conference and the creation of the United Nations.

The particular needs and possibilities of different groups will determine the depth of such studies of the background of the United Nations and its agencies but some time should be devoted to this historical perspective in almost all studies with older students and adults.

Potentialities of the United Nations

The future of the United Nations system is of vital importance to every inhabitant of our planet though the individual may not recognize this fact. Its potentialities are tremendous if the peoples and governments of the world decide to use it as the major inter-governmental instrument for creating a world community based on peace, justice and freedom.

Obviously young children should not be involved in discussions about changes in the United Nations, but they can be encouraged to feel that this organization is important to them and interested in their future. Boys and girls in the upper primary grades can be made aware of the fact that the United Nations and its agencies are breaking the trail on a new frontier in world history and that what its representatives do will help to determine the course of history for many years to come, But they, too, should be spared discussions on the merits and demerits of proposed changes in the United Nations as an organization.

More mature secondary school students, college and university students, and adults should grapple with the problem of the future of the United Nations and its agencies. They need not necessarily come to conclusions on the steps to be taken to increase or decrease its power or change its basic structure but they should examine its present status and possible future realistically. No matter what their conclusions they should be better informed citizens regarding the United Nations, as a result of their deliberations. There are many points of view on the future of the United Nations which can be explored but we shall limit ourselves here to five. It should be borne in mind, however, that there are variations of opinion even within these five general categories.

Relatively few people in the world today, and no governments, would abolish the United Nations entirely. But there is a vigorous, and often very vocal, group which feels strongly that the United Nations already has too much power and that its activities should be severely limited. Some of these critics of the United Nations consider it too good a sounding board for their opponents in the Cold War or charge it with being dominated by their enemies in the world-wide ideological struggle of today. Others feel it is a threat to the sovereignty of their nation, and they would therefore curb its power and its activities. Still others claim that it is too costly and wasteful in its use of funds. People and groups who hold these and similar views are often aware of the potentialities of the United Nations and its agencies but prefer these not to be developed.

A second point of view is that the United Nations is in general satisfactory, but that what is needed is for its members to live up to the purposes outlined in the Charter of the United Nations, and to use the organization more effectively. Many in this general group feel that, in the present state of the world, the best that can be hoped for is the continuation of the United Nations as it is now constituted. They caution against any changes now as upsetting to the equilibrium of the organization. A third point of view is that some changes are needed but that these can be brought about through interpretations of the existing Charter, through regular amendment procedures and through improvements in the functioning of the organization.

A fourth point of view presented by some individuals, groups and governments is that drastic changes are needed. Many of these proponents of change maintain that a general review of the Charter should have been made in 1955 when it was possible to do so according to its provisions. These people, for a variety of reasons, believe that a Charter Review Conference should definitely be held in 1965 or even that sweeping changes should be made before that time. The changes suggested are quite different in scope depending on the views of those challenging the effectiveness of the present organization. One of the most far reaching proposals calls for the establishment of a tripartite executive, a plan submitted by the Government of the U.S.S.R. in 1960. A fifth group goes much farther in its thinking. Its supporters point to the lack of power of the United Nations to enforce its decisions and assert that nothing short of limited world government will suffice to prevent wars, establish better living standards in greater freedom, and establish peace and justice throughout our globe. They consider the present organization weak, ineffective and archaic, and maintain that a much more powerful structure is needed. Although small in number this group is a vigorous and vocal one in the espousal of its cause.

No one can forecast with any certainty the future role of the United Nations and its agencies but a careful review of the five positions outlined above should certainly round out any comprehensive study of the United Nations by mature students in secondary schools, by college and university students and by adults.

3   Some common weaknesses in teaching about the United Nations and its related agencies

Eighteen years have passed since the formation of the United Nations and most of its related agencies and since the first resolutions were passed by the United Nations and Unesco urging their Member States to introduce studies of the United Nations system in their schools. During that period much progress has been made. As the 1960 report to the Economic and Social Council points out :

During recent years public interest in the work of the United Nations and the Specialized Agencies, particularly the interest of educational authorities and of teachers, has grown considerably ; and, in most countries, teaching about the subject in schools and other educational institutions has been extended and improved. As a whole, the record of progress is substantial.

Yet there are several nations today in which there is little or no teaching about the United Nations and its agencies and many in which the teaching is meagre or marginal. Almost everywhere there is room for improvement.

The reasons for lack of teaching or lack of adequate teaching are many. The United Nations system itself is relatively new and teaching about it still newer. Introducing a new topic or theme in many school systems is difficult. The difficulties are increased by the rapid changes in the United Nations and the flexible nature of many of its programmes. There are weaknesses, too, in such studies that do not exist in many of the well-established subjects in the curricula of schools. We shall concentrate here on the negative factors and in the next chapter outline the characteristics of effective programmes, stressing more positive aspects of such teaching.

In the writer's opinion the following are among the many weaknesses in teaching about the United Nations.

Lack of awareness of its importance

In a statement submitted to the Secretary-General of the United Nations in February 1960, the World Federation of United Nations Associations refers to this point by affirming that: 'In its attempts to widen the understanding of the United Nations, one of the main obstacles that WFUNA has encountered is the existence of a discrepancy, varying from country to country, between the urgent need for international co-operation and the official and public awareness of that need.' This report further states that 'The peoples of the world must learn to understand the implications of this knowledge (about the United Nations and its agencies) as well as the repercussions of contemporary life on the development of the international community.'

In a joint statement to the twenty-first International Conference on Public Education held in Geneva, Switzerland, in July 1958, the Secretary-General of the United Nations and the Director General of Unesco declared that '. . . much remains to be done if all school children are to have an opportunity to learn about the United Nations and the Specialized Agencies'. In elaborating this point of view they reported that 'it must be recognized that continued progress in teaching about the United Nations requires that some suitable provision be made for it in the school curriculum'. The importance of a provision for teaching about the United Nations in Member States was further underlined by the 1960 report to the Economic and Social Council pointing out that 'where the rigidity of the educational pattern precludes any change, a reappraisal at the national level would seem to be called for'.

The first obstacle to teaching about the United Nations system that should be overcome is an unawareness on the part of key officials responsible for schools of the extreme importance of the United Nations and its agencies in today's world. Without such an awareness and without proper measures to promote teaching, taken by the top administrative personnel, further progress will be impeded.

Too little time devoted to it

Even where the top officials in national ministries of education approve of teaching about the United Nations family too little time is usually provided for adequate studies of this far-reaching organization. Most countries stage observances of United Nations Day and some of United Nations Week. A good many celebrate other special occasions as well such as Human Rights Day and World Health Day. But the observance of special days no matter how effective, cannot serve as a substitute for full-fledged, comprehensive programmes on the United Nations as outlined in the next chapter.

It is true that this is a new subject and that the curricula of all school systems are already crowded. But teaching about the United Nations and its related agencies is far more important than much now taking priority over it in many schools in the world. Undoubtedly this is what the 1960 report meant in its reference to a 'reappraisal at the national level', as quoted above.

Lack of knowledge as to how to include it in a variety of subject fields

Far too often study of the United Nations system is considered as another subject to be added to the curriculum. Hence there is resistance to its inclusion in already crowded programmes. In fact, almost everyone concerned with such teaching does not consider it a separate study. Educational experts in almost every part of the world believe that students should have some compact, comprehensive treatment of the United Nations family two or three times during their school years. They also believe that much of the most effective teaching about the United Nations can be carried on in existing subjects and without radically modifying existing courses. This obstacle to effective teaching could be overcome by suggestions on ways in which the United Nations and its agencies can be included in present courses. Several such suggestions will appear later in this book.

Lack of background on the part of teachers

Unless teachers know a great deal about the United Nations, they will be fearful of including references to it in their regular work or tackling more comprehensive studies of it. Tremendous gains have been made in recent years in informing teachers, but much remains to be done. Learning about the United Nations should be a normal part of the preparation of teachers, yet in many cases teacher training institutions make little or no specific provision for it and where courses on the United Nations are provided they are rarely obligatory. Efforts to educate prospective teachers and experienced teachers need to be continued and increased in order to remove this road-block to teaching about the United Nations system.

Lack of adequate materials

While there has been some progress, the lack of resources for teaching, especially pictures and material for younger children, is still great and constitutes another serious difficulty in carrying out effective teaching about the United Nations. Solutions to fit particular educational needs and conditions have yet to be worked out. International organizations such as the United Nations and Unesco can help in limited ways—for example, by making available information on the United Nations and on promising teaching methods used in schools in different countries, or by encouraging the exchange of syllabuses, materials and information through the United Nations Information Centres or activities such as the Unesco Associated Schools Project. But it is clear that the preparation, production and distribution of teaching materials must remain primarily a task for the countries themselves.

Lack of comprehensive and balanced programmes

The easiest way to teach about the United Nations system is to concentrate on its structure, but this is certainly not the best way. Such emphasis gives children and young people the skeleton but not the flesh and blood which makes the United Nations come alive. Another tempting approach is to talk about or study the political issues handled by the Security Council and the General Assembly and to limit teaching largely to this phase of the United Nations work. Important though this is, good studies of the United Nations should include at least as much concentration on the work of the Economic and Social Council and the Specialized Agencies, in order to give a balanced picture. A third approach which is enticing is to teach about the United Nations as part of current events. This method seems to have merit but without some opportunities to gain background on the entire system, it gives students a warped view of the United Nations, leading them to believe it is solely concerned with controversies.

Failure to present a variety of points of view

Many of the issues and problems handled by the United Nations and its related agencies are complex and involved. The truth is often very difficult to ascertain even by those who are relatively objective in their thinking and are authorities on the subject. It would seem wise for teachers to ensure that a variety of points of view on controversial issues is presented. On the other hand it is unwise for students, especially children, to try to solve in a few minutes of class discussion issues for which experts have not been able to find suitable solutions over period of months or even years.

Presenting the United Nations as a Super-State

As we pointed out in Chapter 2 of this book, many people seem to think that the United Nations is a very powerful government, playing a role internationally similar to that of governments nationally. A careful reading of the Charter should suffice to clear up this point, but it persists nevertheless in some parts of the world and constitutes another hazard for realistic teaching about the United Nations system.

*Presenting the United Nations as a
very expensive undertaking*

Many people also think that the United Nations system is a very expensive undertaking, costing billions of dollars each year. Actually the regular gross budget for 1961 was approximately $73 million. From this could be deducted a little over $12 million which comes to the United Nations in revenue. Two other large items not included in this figure are the cost of the United Nations Emergency Force in the Gaza Strip, about $17 million, and the cost of the Congo operation, which was over $120 million. Some idea of how relatively small these figures are can be obtained by comparing them with the cost of items for defence. For example, the cost of a nuclear submarine is around $90 million. In the United States, which pays approximately one-third of most of the budgets of the United Nations and its agencies, the total cost of the regular budget of the United Nations per person per year is 70 cents.

Conclusion

These seem to be the main weaknesses in teaching about the United Nations system. An awareness of them should not discourage people from such teaching but should make them more cautious in some of their statements and more realistic in their approach.

Let us now turn to the analysis of an effective programme for studying the United Nations family.

4

Ways to improve teaching about the United Nations and its agencies

If every citizen of the countries belonging to the United Nations and its agencies is to become informed about the United Nations family and actively support its efforts to promote a better world, then schools everywhere and a wide range of out-of-school agencies must plan for more extensive, thorough, and far more imaginative programmes than have been carried out so far, beyond the progress that has been made in the eighteen years of the United Nations' existence. Since it is the schools that must carry the major responsibility for such studies, we shall be concentrating on their task but many of the suggestions made below can be carried out with some adaptation by other organizations.

In the opinion of the author, at least ten clearly-defined types of action, classified under the following headings, could be taken to improve teaching about the United Nations.

Spreading teaching cumulatively over a period of years

The United Nations and its agencies today represent a vast and complex system of organizations working on a host of world-wide problems. Their work is so widespread and complicated that it cannot be treated adequately in one assembly programme a year on United Nations Day of even in a week of special assemblies. Nor will a series of lessons at one grade level suffice to do justice to these organizations. The United Nations system is also of such importance that its study should not be limited to the intellectually gifted or academically inclined. It is a subject worthy of study by everyone attending school and by those millions of children and adults who, though without the advantages of formal education, can yet be reached by out-of-school agencies. Besides, there are enough subjects to examine and projects to analyse to prevent undue repetition in any school programme dealing with the United Nations family. The variety of topics is such that they cannot all be examined in one subject field in any one school or school system.

What is needed, therefore, is a continuous programme for all students. Those in charge of the educational system of any country, or of small units within the country, should take a look at the entire school system and plan broad programmes, starting early and extending over a long period, for all boys and girls and young people. Every subject should be examined to see how it lends itself to a study of the United Nations and its agencies, for although the social sciences or social studies will undoubtedly bear most of the burden of this teaching, almost every subject field can include some work on it. Moreover extra-curricular or co-curricular activities such as those carried out in clubs, assemblies and libraries can play a leading role in helping pupils to learn about the United Nations.

In a few of the reports of Member States in 1960 there is evidence that countries have examined their teaching on the United Nations and its agencies. For example, the Australian report states that 'The belief is commonly held in Australian schools that the study of the United Nations should not be regarded as an independent subject but should arise naturally in the course of teaching about a number of associated topics'; and the reports of Sweden and the United States indicate that teaching is carried on at several levels and in several subjects. But in many of the reports it would seem that teaching on this broad topic is marginal or peripheral and limited to a few students in one or two subjects for very restricted periods of time.

Clarifying objectives

Closely allied to the first characteristic of an effective curriculum on teaching about the United Nations system is the need for clarity of aims. School systems and individual schools should certainly have decided by now that, in today's world, teaching about the United Nations and its agencies should have a high priority. Viet-Nam refers, for example, to the 'special place' accorded to such instruction and Denmark comments on the 'prominent place' given to study of the United Nations, but several countries report that they are still considering the inclusion of such teaching in their schools and others report only a small amount. In the 1960 report no country detailed its aims or referred to any study of the reasons for carrying out such instruction. No doubt many countries and groups of teachers have examined this aspect of their programme but have not reported their findings. In future reports it would be very helpful to have their conclusions summarized. Ministries of Education, teachers' organizations, and individual teachers would certainly find such studies of great value in strengthening existing and proposed programmes on this teaching.

Stressing feelings as well as facts, attitudes as well as knowledge

There is certainly a large body of knowledge which informed citizens should acquire to understand the place of the United Nations and its agencies in the world today, and the importance of which no one can deny. Selecting from the wealth of possible information the essentials for people of various ages is very necessary in any effective programme on the United Nations system. But facts alone will not do the job. People do not support an organization merely because they know about it. They support it because they agree with its aims and have developed a sense of identification with it. They realize its relation to their lives and feel that their present and future well-being are bound up with it. So it is, too, with the United Nations. Facts? Yes. Many of them, carefully selected for their relevance to students. But there should be considerable attention, as well, to the education of feelings and the development of attitudes towards the United Nations and its agencies. As we have pointed out earlier, we stress this approach in education for nationalism but have not paid much attention to this aspect in education for living in the international community of our times.

One of the few reports mentioning this topic is from France which says that 'the principle followed is that education for international understanding and co-operation requires not only the communication of knowledge but also the development of attitudes through the action of the school as a whole'. The United Kingdom's report refers to the analysis of tests given to students, stating that they revealed 'a marked improvement in the pupils' attitudes towards Asian people and an even greater interest and improvement in their attitudes towards the activities of the United Nations and its specialized agencies'. Apparently this is a characteristic of effective curricula which has not been closely examined by those responsible for most educational systems. It, too, merits considerable thought on the part of those carrying out programmes on the United Nations.

Utilizing the findings of research on the learning process

Over the past fifty years there has been a great deal of research on the teaching-learning process. As a result of such studies, we know today a great deal about the conditions under which learning takes place. We know fairly well how people grasp ideas most quickly and retain them for the longest possible period. Some would refer to these findings of research as the fundamental laws of learning. Others would merely maintain that they are guides to effective learning. Whatever term is applied, these findings should be utilized in programmes on the United Nations as in other studies in schools and in non-school organizations.

For example, we know that people learn best when a new learning is related to an older learning. In studies of the United Nations this would mean that comparisons and contrasts be made frequently between the United Nations and the governments of local communities and nations. The analogies are not usually close but students can grasp more about the functioning of the United Nations and its agencies if these are studied in the light of their previous knowledge of other governmental institutions. It is clear, too, that people learn best when learning is reinforced by meaningful repetition. This would probably mean that students consider the subject several times during their school years, usually with different approaches at different age levels.

It is generally accepted that people learn best when they are challenged within the range of their abilities. This would imply a careful examination of the content and methods to be used at different levels of maturity on the part of students, hence a cumulative programme as already mentioned. It is also generally accepted that people learn best through concrete, realistic, and if possible, first-hand experience. This ideal may not be possible in most studies of the United Nations and its agencies but where students can take part in model assemblies, role-playing situations, and dramatic presentations, they are likely to learn faster and retain longer the knowledge acquired. If first-hand experiences are not feasible a great deal of use of audio-visual methods is likely to produce optimum results. People also learn best when they are stimulated emotionally as well as intellectually. This implies using dynamic people who have worked with the United Nations, films on the United Nations' activities which are dramatic and realistic, and similar experiences that have emotional overtones as well as factual value. Another way people learn best is when they take at least some part in selecting the problems to be studied. This will not always be possible but where students can work on special problems of interest to them, individually or in small groups, they are likely to be more interested and to retain longer the information they discover for themselves through research rather than that which they read in textbooks or are given by teachers. Similarly, people learn best when they have opportunities to take some concrete action based on new learning. This would mean that in effective programmes on the United Nations activities be provided in which students could contribute, if only in a small way, to some United Nations project, whether it concerns the United Nations Children's Fund or aid to a refugee family in the local community.

People concerned with effective learning will certainly want to apply these and other findings of the extensive research on learning to the highly important study of the United Nations and its related agencies. The only direct reference to the application of such laws or rules of learning found in the 1960 report is in the Danish account where mention is made of the need for adjusting teaching to the capabilities and maturity of children and young people and for stressing the practical results of United Nations activities rather than its structure. Undoubtedly the teachers of many nations are already applying some of these principles in their day-to-day teaching about the United Nations, but there is unquestionably room for improvement.

Using a wide variety of methods

It is apparent to anyone who has worked with children and young people that there is no one way to reach all of them. The interest of some will be aroused by a speaker. Others become interested because of a book they have read. Still others may have their appetite for learning whetted by a radio or television programme, or a film. It is fairly obvious that all the aims of teaching about the United Nations and its agencies cannot be achieved through any one method. Effective programmes should include therefore a wide variety of methods. This is an aspect of a total programme which will be developed in considerable detail later in this book but it must be mentioned here as another principle in any effective plan for teaching about the United Nations family of organizations.

Employing a wide variety of resources

What has been said in the preceding section about methods applies equally well to the use of resources. A truly effective programme will use as wide a variety of resources as possible including maps, globes, charts, pictures, books, pamphlets and people. This idea will also be developed in the penultimate section of this book, and is merely mentioned at this point as a method of effective teaching.

It is often true that students are pressed too hard by teachers to learn things for which they are not yet ready but it is also true that students' capabilities are often underestimated. When they are faced with realistic problems and challenged to the full, they can often wrestle with complex problems in an astounding way. Studies of the United Nations and its agencies should present such challenges to students in secondary schools and in colleges and universities. If they help select the problems on which they are to work and see the relevance of these problems to their lives today and tomorrow, they can think realistically and clearly, under capable leadership. Programmes should provide opportunities for such rigorous and clear thinking at least as much as programmes about other topics in the curricula of schools.

Ensuring the adequate preparation of teachers

It is evident that most governments are aware of the importance of the training of teachers if adequate programmes on the United Nations and its agencies are to be undertaken in schools. This topic was treated by many countries in the 1960 report. It will be dealt with elsewhere at greater length as it is probably the keystone of any effective programme. Any analysis of a programme in a school, a school system or a nation should certainly include this as one of the most important.

Including experimentation and evaluation

Despite some very fine work, the topic of teaching about the United Nations and its agencies is still largely unexplored territory. There are many opportunities for experimentation on the age at which this subject can best be introduced, the most effective methods in presenting different aspects of it, and the means of evaluating learning on this broad theme. Perusal of the literature on the subject reveals almost nothing about the process of evaluating such teaching. Tests of factual information exist here and there but tests of attitudes towards the United Nations are few. Enterprising educators might well turn their attention to this relatively unknown field of research and through their efforts help thousands of classroom teachers around the world.

Enlisting administrative and community support and co-operation

Classroom teachers need the active support of administrators in teaching about the United Nations and its agencies. This is true both in countries with highly centralized school systems and in those with decentralized systems. Teachers not only need to be told that they should teach about the United Nations, they also need to be encouraged to do so, and they need to have suggestions from their superiors as to methods and materials. In places where the importance of teaching about the United Nations is still questioned, there is also a need for community support. Administrators would do well to interpret the programmes in their schools to the general public and to arouse and maintain active support for them. Since schools cannot possibly do the entire job themselves, there should be active co-operation with various community organizations that work with out-of-school youth and adults, so that the total effort of a community on this subject can be co-ordinated. Often the schools and other community agencies can pool their resources and co-operate in the use of speakers, the showing of films, the planning of exhibitions and the launching of projects, thus helping all the parties concerned to do a more effective job.

There is considerable evidence in the 1960 report that administrative support is being given in many parts of the world to programmes for teaching about the United Nations and its related agencies. There is also some evidence that the schools of several countries are working with other agencies to improve community-wide programmes. Examples will be cited in other parts of this book; they are mentioned here as an indication of the progress which has been made in the last few years in many countries on this final method of effective teaching.

Conclusion

Individual teachers, groups of teachers, the staffs of schools and school systems, members of school boards and local educational authorities, and members of national ministries of education would undoubtedly find it profitable to ask these questions with regard to teaching about the United Nations and its agencies:

1. Is there a comprehensive, continuous, cumulative programme?
2. Are there clear aims for this programme?
3. Are feelings as well as facts, attitudes as well as knowledge stressed?
4. Are the findings of research on the learning process used?
5. Are a wide variety of methods and resources used?
6. Is rigorous and clear thinking on the part of students encouraged?
7. Is the adequate preparation of teachers encouraged?
8. Are experimentation and evaluation included as integral parts of the programme?
9. Is there administrative and community support and co-operation in fostering study of the United Nations and its agencies?

A careful examination of these questions by educators would certainly do much to improve teaching about the United Nations in every school, school system, and country of the world. It is hoped that many will find them helpful in evaluating their programmes.

5 Suggestions for implementing a comprehensive programme on the United Nations and its agencies

It should be clear from the foregoing that teaching about the United Nations and its agencies is not to be disposed of by the celebration of United Nations Day or Week or a few pages in a textbook for secondary school students. Nor can it be treated adequately in a single grade or subject. What is needed in all school systems is a planned programme from the early years in school up to and including institutions of higher learning, with the scope and sequence clearly indicated. There must also be an equally well planned programme for children, youth and adults not reached by the formal institutions of learning.

To develop such programmes will take time, the best thinking of many people (including classroom teachers) and the experience of educators in all parts of the world. Various countries have stressed various aspects of such a comprehensive programme. By examining their experiences, we should all profit from their findings. In this chapter, therefore, we intend to make a quick survey of the current practices in teaching about the United Nations system, starting with the early years in school, moving up the educational ladder through institutions of higher learning, and going on to out-of-school and adult education programmes.

In the early years at school

Many educators today feel that direct teaching about the United

Nations is inappropriate and even unwise in the pre-primary and primary grades. Several people and organizations took exception to the statement in an early Unesco publication that some parts of the United Nations might be studied by boys and girls from 7 to 9 years of age. C. F. Strong, in a booklet on *Teaching for International Understanding*, prepared for the United Kingdom National Commission for Unesco, declared that such an approach was a 'misconception' of education and stated that 'we wish to make it clear that we do not find such a view acceptable'.[1] A similar publication, prepared by the Council for Education in World Citizenship in the United Kingdom states that 'We consider that in general it is neither possible nor desirable to give children under the age of 12 direct teaching on the United Nations'.[2] This view seems to be shared by educators in several countries, for reports reveal that very little is being taught on this topic in the first three years of school.

Perhaps this point of view needs to be re-examined in the light of our rapidly changing world. Opposition to teaching about the United Nations and its agencies in the first years of school is based largely on the belief that children should be introduced first to their neighbourhood, then to the community, a little later to the larger region within the nation, and finally to their nation. Only after all these societies have been studied, should children be introduced to the world. But are the facts behind this belief valid today? Are contacts with the world postponed until a child is 11 or 12? Is knowledge about the destructive power of supersonic missiles and man's attempt to reach the moon limited to adults in the 1960s? Are children unaware of the United Nations and its agencies today? Is it not true that in many parts of the world radio and television today bring the world into the homes o children even before they enter school and that films portray people abroad and even refer sometimes to the conflicts and controversies with which the United Nations is wrestling? Are there not millions of boys and girls today who receive or have

1. C. F. Strong, op. cit.
2. *Teaching about the United Nations*, London, Council for Education in World Citizenship, undated, p. 5.

received aid from one of the agencies of the United Nations? And thousands upon thousands of children who have seen United Nations representatives at work on some phase of the extensive technical assistance programme? Is it not true that even young children learn these days about the emergence of new nations and the efforts of the United Nations to bring peace and stability to the Congo? And that there are millions of children living near ports and airports where they see people from all over the world? Probably most educators everywhere would agree that the local community should be the focus for teaching in the pre-primary and primary grades. They are unanimous or nearly unanimous in their contention that teaching about other lands in the early years should concentrate on people and their ways of living, stressing that everywhere they carry on the same human activities but in different ways in different parts of the world. But does this rule out teaching about some aspects of the United Nations and its agencies in the early years in school? When the report on this subject was presented to the Economic and Social Council in 1960, Santha Rama Rau, speaking (in the absence of Mrs. Eleanor Roosevelt) for the World Federation of United Nations Associations, took exception to the statement that teaching about the United Nations was 'beyond the grasp of children at the pre-school and lower primary stages'. She testified to the contrary that the 'experience of WFUNA has shown that it is frequently easier to teach about the United Nations in the primary grades' and pointed out that since most of the world's children never go beyond the primary grades, it is 'vital' to begin such teaching quite early.

This comment raises another question. What should be done about the millions of children who drop out after two or three years of school? They may be reached eventually by some of the out-of-school programmes attempting to explain and interpret the United Nations' place in their lives and in the lives of others but the chances for a school programme to reach them are far greater. This problem was emphasized in a joint statement by the Secretary-General of the United Nations and the Director-General of Unesco to the twenty-first International Conference on Public Education. They said: 'It is perhaps especially important that such teaching be carried out at the primary level, since most of the world's children who go to school receive no formal education beyond this point, and also since the basic principles about the world order in which we live should be learned at this stage.'[1] Hence, it is important to consider which aspects of the United Nations should be taught in schools before many children leave never to return.

One may also ask why it is important to begin educating children for support of their national community even before they enter school and yet postpone education for support of their international community until they are 11 or 12. In every nation young children are encouraged to attend parades and celebrations honouring their nation, sing songs about their country, listen to stories about their national heroes and hear simple accounts of their nation's past. Adults believe that boys and girls are thus initiated into the national community. Is it not equally important to initiate them through similar experiences into the international community in which they will spend their lives? Should they not attend parades and celebrations, sing songs, and listen to stories about the United Nations and its component parts, whether they understand intellectually the full implications of this international organization or not? The disagreement as to how early some teaching should be introduced may be due partly to disagreement on the meaning of the words 'direct' and 'indirect' and partly to differences in philosophy on the role of schools. But there should be much to gain from discussions in many areas of the world on the type of activities that can be carried on effectively with young children and the age at which children can be introduced to the United Nations and/or its agencies.

Having posed this question it is perhaps in order for the writer to suggest briefly some aspects which might be taught. Speaking negatively, it is obvious that at an early age there should be no teaching about the structure of the United Nations and, except in instances where children are directly involved in conflicts and

1. Teaching about the United Nations: a Statement by the Secretary-General of the United Nations and the Director-General of Unesco, twenty-first International Conference on Public Education, 7-16 July 1958.

controversies that it is handling, there should be no discussions of involved problems. Every effort should be made to introduce children at this stage of their development to a non-threatening world. There are enough threats to their security without adding problems which do not touch them and about which they can do nothing. Nor should there be any place in early schooling for the study of difficult statements in the United Nations Charter and the constitutions of its agencies.

Speaking positively, children should be able to grasp the main concept that adults are trying to make this a better world, especially for children. Millions of them know what it is to be hungry and poor, live in bad houses, be ill, and not go to school. They need to know that people in many parts of the world are concerned with such conditions and are trying to do something about them. There are often examples of United Nations projects in local or nearby communities that can be used. Pictures, films, filmstrips and other visual materials can show the efforts of adults to build a better world for children as well as for themselves. Stories can be told, and eventually included in textbooks, that illustrate the efforts being made to provide better food, better medical care, more and better schools and better agriculture. Children learn very early that older people have problems and do not always solve them by peaceful methods. They learn that people have fought in the past and are still fighting in some parts of the world because they disagree. It is good for them to realize that people know how destructive and harmful wars are and that they are trying to do something to prevent them.

Young children can participate in local celebrations of United Nations Day and Week, World Health Day and other similar events. They may even have class or school parties of their own to celebrate the birthday of the United Nations, learning in a very simple way what it is trying to do. This is not a strong intellectual approach, but education should pay attention to the development of emotions as well as intellects. Some simple study can also be made of the work of the Universal Postal Union in helping to transmit letters across the world; of the Food and Agriculture Organization and its efforts to improve farming and fishing; and of the World Health Organization and its attempts to improve the health of millions of people, including children. The most appropriate part of the United Nations for the very young to study is Unicef, the United Nations Children's Fund, since its work is almost solely concentrated on children. Some schools may want to fly the United Nations flag in the school or in classrooms and interpret it to children as a symbol of the world-wide family of three thousand million persons.

What we are trying to suggest is that there is a readiness programme in international affairs just as there are readiness programmes, for reading, writing, arithmetic and civics. It is a possibility worth exploring.

In the upper primary or middle grades

There is general agreement that this teaching can usefully be carried out with children from 10 or 11 to 14 or 15 years of age. As school systems vary so greatly and there is no terminology to describe them all, we shall refer to this age-group as the upper primary or middle grades, using the terms interchangeably.

Many countries have provided teaching about the United Nations in these grades for several years with considerable success. None of them stated in the 1960 report that it had dropped or curtailed such studies. Some nations in fact reported that they had increased them. Yugoslavia, for instance, said that it had extended its teaching in 1958 to this general level and Ghana stated that its new history syllabus for the sixth year included a series of lessons on 'Ghana and the United Nations'. In Israel the eighth and ninth grade geography course now contains material on the United Nations and is required of all students. The United States reported wide acceptance of teaching about the United Nations and its related agencies in these middle grades and the publication of many suitable books, booklets and other teaching materials. Since a large percentage of students in most countries drop out of school at 14 or 15, it is highly important that considerable attention be given to the United Nations before then. The increased maturity of students and their increased ability to read makes such studies at this stage of their school careers more feasible than in the early primary years.

In the first years of this period in school students should learn about the United Nations and its agencies through numerous references to it as they study a variety of topics. The Australian report states this general approach well when it says that 'the study of the United Nations should not be regarded as an independent subject but should arise naturally in the course of teaching about a number of associated topics'. Most schools, for example, teach about food, clothing, transport and communications, health and housing in the upper primary or middle grades. At various points in these studies students should be confronted with the work of the United Nations and its agencies in improving transport and communications, in attacking disease and taking preventive measures to improve health, in assisting farmers to improve their agricultural methods and to increase food supplies, and in helping nations to build ports, railroads, radio and television stations. Stories of practical action in building a better world should be stressed and much visual material incorporated to make these stories vivid to students. Some attention can be given to current events in which the United Nations figures prominently but students should not be urged to try to solve in a few minutes, or even in a few days, problems with which adults have wrestled for weeks and months and years. If they do study some of the current problems of the United Nations, they should be led to see the variety of points of view and the difficulty of reaching agreement on any problem. In these grades boys and girls often like to dramatize the stories they have read and much use should be made of this special interest. As students begin to study geography, either as a separate course or as part of a broad social studies programme, they can investigate how the United Nations is working in the countries they are studying and the part that these countries play in the United Nations and its agencies. In this way geography and the study of the United Nations are integrated and the effectiveness of the teaching should be enhanced.

In the more industrialized nations, with higher standards of living, extreme care should be taken to avoid the characterization of the United Nations as a charitable organization aiding the poorer nations of the world. Over and over the theme should be stressed of nations sharing their skills. At some stage in these grades, almost every student takes a course in civics or government, whether it is designated by that term or not. Many teachers may want to compare the United Nations with the local and national governments that have been studied. If this is done, care should be taken to show that it lacks the power these units have and to point out that it is not a world government. It is misleading and even dangerous, for example, to equate the General Assembly with the parliamentary bodies of most nations or the International Court of Justice with the highest judicial bodies in almost every country.

Some students may become interested in such specialized agencies as the International Civil Aviation Organization, the International Telecommunication Union or the International Labour Organisation. The nature of their work and the lack of materials for students on these and several other parts of the United Nations system makes them better subjects for individual research than for class treatment. Similarly some may become interested in the work of the regional economic commissions, the Atomic Energy Commission, the Commission on Human Rights or the Commission on Narcotic Drugs, to mention only a few. Many adolescents enjoy biography and in these grades much use should be made of accounts of men and women who have worked or are now working for the United Nations and its specialized agencies.

The possibilities for this teaching in the upper primary or middle grades are numerous and exciting. Imaginative teachers will have little difficulty in finding worthwhile topics to include in their work in a variety of subject fields.

At some point, however, every student should have a more organized study of the entire United Nations system, including the commissions and agencies. This should serve as a review of all that has gone before but should also introduce new material and give students a comprehensive look at the manifold aspects of the United Nations family. Some attention should be given to its structure and that of its agencies, although this should not be stressed. This comprehensive picture is needed especially for those who do not continue their formal schooling after the age of 14 or 15. If the educators of any nation feel that they can devote only a small amount of time to a study of the United Nations, it is probably wise to carry it out in the last year of this period in school.

In secondary schools

The 1960 report painted a brighter picture about teaching in the secondary schools of the world on the United Nations and its agencies than in the earlier grades. The report summarized the present status of such teaching in these words :

It is at the secondary level that teaching about the United Nations family seems to be most widespread and systematic. It has become an established part of the educational programme of secondary schools in many countries, and indications are that it is developing steadily.

The report from the U.S.S.R. states that every student leaving secondary school in that country is familiar with the activities of the United Nations and its specialized agencies.

The 1960 report points out that more attention is still given to this aspect of education in ordinary schools than in specialized ones, but it notes a trend toward more teaching about the United Nations in technical and vocational schools. It is good to know of these trends. They should encourage those who over a period of years have sought to increase the amount and improve the quality of teaching about the United Nations and its related agencies. At the same time much remains to be done.

Unfortunately, in most countries, only a small fraction of students over 14 years of age are in school. It is also evident to people acquainted with teaching about the United Nations that far too much of the learning is confined to a knowledge of the structure and the memorization of a few key facts. Much greater depth is needed and more challenging analyses of its work should be undertaken in many secondary schools now offering instruction on the United Nations family. Better preparation of teachers and much better materials are two ways in which teaching could be improved in the future.

There are several methods in the study of the United Nations and its agencies which can be used at the secondary level rather than attempting them at the upper primary level. One of these is the historical approach. Students at this age are much more aware of the element of time and can study the United Nations in historical perspective, gaining a view of it as the current and most ambitious attempt by men to foster international co-opera- tion. Many schools are already spending some time on a comparison of the League of Nations and the United Nations in order to see how the latter can be made more effective. These and other schools are devoting even more time to the world-wide setting in which the United Nations was established and in which it is now working.

Another commendable approach with this age-group is the study of world problems and the efforts of the United Nations and its agencies to cope with them. This is a highly realistic method and is more conducive to critical thinking than most others. Since this is such a promising practice, more attention will be devoted to it in the section of this booklet on methods and resources. A third approach, more effective with secondary school students than with primary grade pupils, is the study of the structure of the United Nations. To younger students this is largely meaning- less ; to secondary school students it can be quite significant.

More use can be made of current events too, for students of this age have more background to bring to the study of contemporary affairs and are usually more interested in them because of their greater maturity. Some research can be carried out on various aspects of the United Nations and its agencies. The interests of boys and girls of this age are more likely to be clear and teachers can encourage individual research of a simple nature on topics which appeal to them. This requires greater library resources than most schools have but is a method which can be used very effec- tively in some schools. Able students, for example, can be asked to prepare 'position papers' which, if they were members of a permanent civil service, they might be asked to submit to the Foreign Office of their country. Others can be encouraged to delve into the work of the International Bank and the Monetary Fund, the Disarmament Commission or the Population Commission. At this level attention can also be given with profit to suggestions for the strengthening of the United Nations. This is not a topic for individuals not keenly interested in world affairs but it is a good one for students who have considerable background and the ability to tackle involved and difficult subjects.

In thinking about the aims of teaching about the United Nations and its agencies in secondary schools, it is important to bear in mind that almost all such institutions are organized by subject fields. While the bulk of teaching will probably be done in all schools in geography, history, or allied subjects, it must be remembered that the United Nations is not a topic which should be confined to the social sciences. Its study should permeate almost every subject field, especially through incidental teaching.

With this important consideration in mind, let us look at some of the ways in which the United Nations family can be included in various subject fields in secondary schools. No attempt will be made to be exhaustive in dealing with this topic ; examples will be given in a limited number of fields, suggestive of general approaches. Teachers in various parts of the world may want to expand this list and select items which they can translate into action in their own classes. Ministries of Education and teacher organizations may want to expand the list to include other subjects and to develop some of the items in detail. It should be pointed out again that this booklet is on teaching about the United Nations and its agencies and that scores of topics related to the much broader field of education for international understanding are not included.

In science considerable attention can be paid to up-to-date studies of race, with reference to the several publications of Unesco on this topic. The work of the Food and Agriculture Organization can be stressed, especially in farming communities and in countries whose economy is primarily agricultural. The work of the World Health Organization also lends itself to study in science classes, with special attention to health problems in the locality or nation, as they relate to international health problems. Issues of the magazine *World Health* should be invaluable to many science teachers, especially since it is published in English, French, Portuguese, Russian and Spanish.

Much of the work of the Technical Assistance Programme of the United Nations involves science and should be considered an integral part of science teaching. The activities of several of the commissions and committees of the United Nations are also scientific in nature, such as those of the International Atomic Energy Agency, the International Labour Organisation, the Population Commission and the Scientific Committee on the Effects of Atomic Radiation. Many students will be especially interested in the work of the International Labour Organisation on automation and in its publication on that subject.[1] The work of the science section of Unesco is full of appeal to young scientists, and of value to them whether it concerns Unesco's Arid Zones Project or the activities of its Science Field Co-operation Offices. Feature articles on scientific subjects are frequently included in *The Unesco Courier*.

Science teachers have done far too little so far to incorporate the work of the United Nations and its agencies into their class work but there is much that can and should be done in this part of the curricula of secondary schools.

In *language classes* there are also many opportunities. Beginners can gain considerable background on the United Nations while learning another language, by using charts and simple accounts written in any of the five languages used by the United Nations: Chinese, English, French, Spanish and Russian. A few publications have been printed by the United Nations or its agencies in which the same text appears in two or three languages on the same page, giving the beginning students a change to compare the text in a foreign language with the same information in their native tongue. The use of the many films and filmstrips which have appeared with the texts in different languages is another means of promoting language training and education about the United Nations simultaneously.

For more advanced students issues of *The Unesco Courier* in Arabic, English, French, German, Italian, Japanese, Spanish and Russian can serve as useful supplementary materials. The same thing is true regarding other magazines such as the *United Nations Review* and *World Health*. While students are learning a foreign

---

1. *Automation*, Geneva, International Labour Organisation. 26 p., English, French, Spanish. Free on request.

language, they can be assimilating interesting and important information on a host of subjects related to the United Nations and the world. Advanced students can also read with profit some of the documents of the United Nations and its agencies in the language they are learning, or they can try their hand at translating some of these documents.

Two Member States of the United Nations have taken action in this respect. The Japanese Government has issued *A Guide to the United Nations and Unesco* in English for use in language classes in senior high schools and colleges, and the Philippine Government has published a book on *The United Nations and the Philippines* with the text in Tagalog and English on parallel pages.

A useful service to language teachers and students would be the preparation by United Nations interpreters and translators of accounts of their work, including some references to the problems they encounter in their day-to-day assignments. Carefully prepared, this could be a fascinating document for use in language classes as well as in other subject fields. Most of the films produced by the United Nations and its agencies are issued in many language versions and could be used, in addition to written materials, to provide a varied range of resources for language classes.

In *literature classes* considerable study about the United Nations system can be carried on profitably. A few books on the United Nations can be included in reading lists and oral comments, or written summaries and reactions to them can be made by students as part of their regular work. Research papers can be prepared by more mature students as part of their experience in learning the skills connected with research and in learning how to write. Speeches can also be written, such as a talk the President of the General Assembly might give at the opening of the autumn session of the United Nations. In the booklet prepared by the New York City Board of Education, *Toward Better International Understanding*, a section is included for literature classes on 'Human Aspirations in World Literature' that seems particularly appropriate.[1] Speeches made at various meetings of the United Nations

1. New York City Board of Education, *Toward Better International Understanding: A Manual for Teachers*, Brooklyn, New York, Board of Education, 1960, 253 p.

and its agencies can be read or excerpts from them used for reading
or speech work. Mock interviews and dramatizations of outstanding
events should be informative as well as good language training.
In some instances articles on various aspects of the United Nations
can be written for use in school newspapers.

Similar activities can be developed in most of the separate
subject fields offered in the schools of the world. Even in mathe-
matics classes some study and analysis can be made of statistical
information, the budgets of the United Nations and its related
agencies and of problems of international finance. More suggestions
on these lines will be found in Chapter 6 of this booklet. It is hoped
that these will suffice to alert teachers to the different ways in
which the United Nations system can be included in existing
courses of study in a variety of fields.

In institutions of higher education

Some study of the United Nations system should be included in
programmes for men and women in the colleges, universities,
technical institutes and other higher institutions of learning in all
Member States. Such a background is essential to them as effective
citizens and even more important to them as prospective leaders
in their own countries. If this is true for all individuals in these
institutions in highly industrialized nations, it is even more true
for men and women in the industrially underdeveloped countries,
where the number of highly educated individuals is relatively
small and their potential leadership correspondingly greater.

A thorough study of the United Nations should not be considered
an isolated part of their education but a significant part of a much
broader acquaintance with the rapidly-changing and highly-
interdependent world of the latter half of the twentieth century.
Such an ideal was stated briefly and succinctly in the Ford
Foundation report on *The University and World Affairs* issued
in 1960 in the United States. This asserted that 'A first-class
liberal education in the second half of the twentieth century should
unquestionably include an effective international component'.[1]

1. Committee on the University and World Affairs, *The University and World
Affairs*, New York, The Ford Foundation, 1960, p. 17.

Studies of the important United Nations system should be seen as part of the responsibility of officials in institutions of higher learning to provide this 'international component', to help in preparation for living in this chaotic, but nevertheless exciting, period of history.

In the 1960 report it is stated that:

About one-third of the replies from Member States report that teaching about the United Nations is included in courses of study at the university and post-graduate level, and it can be assumed from other evidence that universities in many countries also offer instruction on the subject.

However, the document mentions that not all students take courses devoted exclusively or even partially to a study of the United Nations even when these are offered. Moreover it is evident from the individual reports of nations that a large proportion of the courses are limited to students working in political science, law and international relations. From this it would appear that many colleges and universities need to re-examine their courses in the light of the changed conditions in the world so that many more students have a chance to acquire a relatively deep knowledge of the United Nations system and its role in world affairs today.

There are at least six major aspects of teaching about the United Nations and its agencies which might well be considered by those responsible for the curricula of institutions of higher learning.

One is to provide at least some study of the United Nations for all students as part of their advanced work. In some instances this can be provided within existing courses by changes in their content. In others it may mean the development of new courses of study within current courses or the establishment of separate new courses. In still other cases it can perhaps be provided by a series of public lectures, films and club programmes intended to reach all or nearly all of the students. A second responsibility in this field should be provision for the specific training of some of its students for international work, including the United Nations and its agencies. This might involve very few students in some institutions but it is a service which must be provided in the years ahead to meet the growing demand for well-qualified and well-trained individuals for international posts, many within the United Nations. A third function of higher institutions is to alert faculty members to the opportunities for service abroad, including work with the United Nations, and to make it possible for them to serve where needed. A fourth service which some of these institutions can provide is to carry out research on a variety of world problems, including topics essential to the improved functioning of the United Nations and its specialized agencies. A fifth responsibility is to help the citizens of their communities to become better informed about world affairs in general and the United Nations system in particular. This can be done in a variety of ways, from public lectures to the preparation of reading lists, from seminars and conferences to the loan of audio-visual materials to community organizations and schools, and from the furnishing of speakers and consultants to community organizations and schools to the preparation and display of exhibits dealing with the work of the United Nations. A sixth task is the assistance they can render to faculty members and students from abroad and to visiting scholars and field workers, including United Nations representatives and fellowship holders.

Confronted with new conditions, the institutions of higher learning all over the world can continue to exert leadership only if they are alert to the new tasks that have been thrust upon them. This will usually involve a comprehensive and far-reaching study of their present responsibilities and the need for change, the development of new courses and the strengthening of old ones, the continued training of personnel and recruitment of new personnel, the strengthening of teaching resources, the acquisition of adequate funds, and long-term plans for the development of broad and effective programmes on world affairs, including the United Nations and its specialized agencies.

In teacher-training institutions

An encouraging note is struck in the 1960 report regarding the training of teachers. It summarizes the reports from member states in this way: 'Replies from Member States indicate that in most countries an increased effort is being made to train student teachers and teachers-in-service for work in this field.' On the other hand the report of the World Confederation of Organizations of the Teaching Profession to the Economic and Social Council in that same year states that: 'Only to a very limited extent is formal instruction being given to students in teachers' colleges regarding the work of the United Nations and its specialized agencies.'

Certainly there are wide variations in this respect among the Member States that submitted reports. Ceylon, for example, reports very frankly that 'teaching about the United Nations is handicapped by the dearth of teachers with pre-service training in the subject'. Morocco reports that it plans to establish a course which would include a large section or sections on the United Nations system. At the other end of the spectrum is Mexico which reports that 'full instruction on the aims and work of the United Nations and its related agencies is given in all the teacher-training institutions in the Mexican federal educational system to students preparing to teach in the primary and secondary schools'.

No matter what is being done at present, educators would certainly agree upon the importance of training teachers to carry out instruction about the United Nations system. The education of the prospective teacher and of the experienced teacher are the two most important tasks to stimulate more and better teaching about the United Nations.

Some would go even farther, as did the statement of Mrs. Franklin D. Roosevelt presented to the Economic and Social Council by the World Federation of United Nations Associations on 5 April 1960, in which it was said:

The teacher training institution is the foremost place in which to begin teaching about the United Nations. The young teacher-to-be, anxious to learn, least likely to have formed his or her pattern of teaching, is most likely to see ways of including studies of the United Nations in the courses that he is going to teach, and to see the advantages of teaching subjects of topical and current interest, directly related to problems of international co-operation.

In the report from the Philippine Republic the essentials of a teacher-training programme are put down in detail. Three parts to such a programme are mentioned. One is the general education of the prospective teacher. A second is the inclusion of knowledge of the United Nations in the specific professional preparation of teachers-to-be. A third is the wide use of extra-curricular activities to give future teachers important background information on the United Nations system. Let us examine each of these aspects more closely.

Future teachers need the same kind of general background on the United Nations system as was outlined in the opening paragraphs of the section on institutions of higher learning. In colleges and universities where teachers are educated as members of a much larger student body, they will undoubtedly acquire a background knowledge of world affairs and the United Nations in classes with other students preparing for a variety of careers. In colleges devoted solely to the training of teachers, general courses on world affairs should be an essential part of their training. These should include a sizeable section on the United Nations system. But again, teachers should not see the United Nations system in isolation. They should see it against the general background of these revolutionary times. They should become acquainted with the fact that people are rebelling against colonialism, discrimination, feudalistic land practices, low standards of living, ignorance and illiteracy, war, often against established value systems and sometimes against established forms of economic and political organization. Students should gain a realistic view of some world problems such as the armaments race, the population explosion, prejudice and discrimination, disease, poverty and hunger. Only against such a background will a study of the United Nations be realistic and meaningful and the United Nations eventually be interpreted in the classrooms of these teachers as a dynamic and vital organization facing the pressing problems of the world.

Some institutions acknowledge the need for special courses for teachers on the United Nations and its related agencies. For example, Norway reported fifteen special courses on the United Nations family, arranged by the United Nations Association in various teacher-training colleges during the period from 1956 to 1959, which were attended by a total of 1,800 persons. In a survey of fifty-four institutions of higher learning in the United States which were educating future teachers, 192 courses were mentioned as including some study of the United Nations system. Of these, twenty-nine were devoted exclusively to the United Nations, thirty-eight gave major attention to it, ninety-nine a considerable amount of time to the topic and thirty-seven a small part.

Background material on the United Nations can often be included in special professional courses. This practice was reported by Mexico, with specific reference to courses in the 'History of Education' and in methods of teaching. Occasionally new courses can be offered on an experimental basis, dealing solely or partially with the United Nations system. Such is the case with two new courses offered in Japanese teacher-training institutions. One is 'The Study of Human Rights' and the other 'The Study of South-East Asian Countries', including considerable material on the work of the United Nations in that area. The only country reporting a correspondence course for teachers on the United Nations is Norway. This is a course on Unesco with a text specially prepared for this purpose.

As well as the general background future teachers require on world affairs, they should have specific information about the United Nations and training in ways of teaching about the United Nations system. These may be given in courses on the United Nations family, on teaching about the world or education for international understanding, or in general methods courses, depending upon the interest and competency of the instructors. In connexion with such courses, teachers in training should know the major sources of information and where they can be found. The same applies to teachers in service who will have the added responsibility of obtaining suitable materials for study by their pupils. For general reading, and for reference purposes, many United Nations publications can be used by teachers and students alike. The more important of these are therefore listed later in Chapter 6 of this booklet under the section 'Textbooks and Supplementary Reading Materials'.

In addition to the illustrated periodicals, information pamphlets, annual reports and yearbooks mentioned in Chapter 6, some booklets have been prepared with teachers specifically in mind. Among these is the Unesco series *Towards World Understanding*. This is now out of print but the booklets are often obtainable from libraries. Two titles of interest are No. VIII, *A Teacher's Guide to the Declaration of Human Rights*, and No. XII, *Round the World with a Postage Stamp*, the story of the Universal Postal Union. Another Unesco periodical of interest is the *Education Abstracts* series which includes *Primary Education in Asia; Citizenship Education for Girls;* and *Comparative Education.* Among recent Unesco publications prepared for free distribution and general reading are some of special interest for teachers, for example, *Towards Equality in Education*, a study of discrimination in this field and of international action in the struggle against it, and *Africa Calls*, an illustrated account of the needs and problems in education of developing countries in Africa.

Practical examples of units and activities designed for teaching about the United Nations within the broader field of education for international understanding are given in a United Nations booklet *Teaching for Human Rights* and a Unesco booklet *Education for International Understanding: Examples and Suggestions for Classroom Use*, both of which appear in English, French and Spanish. The first contains 'A Lesson on the Rights of Man' taken from a report of the French Ministry of Education, two simplified versions of the Universal Declaration of Human Rights prepared by children in the Philippines and the United States, and an account of 'Teaching about the Rights of Women in Ecuador' among other examples of classroom and extra-curricular projects.

Recent publications especially designed for assistance to students, youth groups and teachers are the first two volumes in a series on the United Nations and its agencies issued by the Oceana Library on the United Nations, New York. The material for the booklets was assembled by the Unesco Youth Institute in co-operation with the United Nations. Volume 1, *World Peace and the United Nations*, covers three aspects of United Nations work: collective security, the rule of law and the International Court of Justice and work for refugees. Volume 2, *Food for Life—Food for Thought*, is a study of two United Nations agencies, the Food and Agriculture Organization and Unesco. Volumes in preparation are on WHO, ILO, Technical Assistance and peaceful uses of atomic energy. A third booklet published by this library is *How to Plan and Conduct Model UN Meetings*. It was prepared by the United Nations in co-operation with Unesco in response to an increasing number of requests for information about model sessions which have come from many different countries. The World Federation of United Nations Associations, as part of its contribution to teaching about the United Nations regularly publishes pamphlets and teachers' manuals on subjects of interest. *Disarmament*, a study guide and bibliography on the efforts of the United Nations in this field, was published in 1958: *The Universal Declaration of Human Rights*, published in 1961, is a collection of essays based on talks given at the twelfth annual WFUNA Summer School held in Geneva.

Lists of currently available materials can be obtained free on request from the United Nations, from information services of its related agencies and from their official sales agents in many countries. Also, some national bodies, particularly the United Nations Associations in many countries, have produced useful lists and bibliographies.

Future teachers might well view and note their reactions to a number of films on the United Nations system mentioned in Chapter 6 of this book,[1] as well as see several films and filmstrips dealing specifically with the educational activities of Unesco and Unicef. Among the films in this latter category are *World Without End* ; *Assignment Children*, a pictorial account of the round the world trip of Danny Kaye, the film star, to meet the children of the world and to see what Unicef is doing for them ; and *When the Mountains Move*, an account of radio education in Colombia. The filmstrip *The UN in Asia* produced by Unesco and available in English, French and Spanish, might usefully be included.

Teachers in training should also have some opportunity to examine and evaluate the materials they will probably use with

---

1. See also *Films of the United Nations Family*, New York, United Nations, 1961, 91 p. $0.25, 1/6 (stg.), 1 Sw.Fr. A comprehensive annotated catalogue which lists and describes the films produced by the United Nations and its related agencies.

boys and girls and young people. These will be referred to in more detail in Chapter 6. They should also study at least one topic dealing with the United Nations system in some depth. This could be one of the specialized agencies or one of the United Nations Commissions, or a problem with which the United Nations is currently dealing. They might well prepare at least one visual aid of their own on the United Nations which they could take with them to their first job. It would be helpful if every one of these future teachers could be supplied with a kit of materials on the United Nations, provided by his government, by the United Nations Association of his country of by some other organization. This would do much to ensure better teaching. Such kits or folders of materials are among the most useful devices to have been developed. References are made to them in the reports from the United Kingdom and from Germany in the 1960 report and they are used widely in some other countries. The reference in the United Kingdom's report is to kits prepared by the Council for Education in World Citizenship. They include pamphlets produced by the United Nations and its agencies, lists of visual aids available in the United Kingdom, and suggested courses and programmes of study. All these are contained in a sturdy folder.

Through help to teachers in service[1]

Effective teaching about the United Nations system cannot be delayed until a new generation of teachers is produced, informed and interested in this aspect of teaching. Millions of people who are teaching at present must be trained so that they can contribute to dynamic instruction about the United Nations family. This is a pressing need and it is encouraging to see the many references to it in the 1960 report. Obviously many school systems and non-governmental organizations are concerned about the in-service education of teachers and are taking action to foster better

1. For general suggestions on the training of teachers in service see Recommendation No. 55 adopted at the twenty-fifth session of the International Conference on Public Education convened jointly by Unesco and the International Bureau of Education, Geneva, July 1962.

teaching. There are scores of ways in which in-service education about the United Nations can be carried on. Lack of space limits us to a few of the most promising.

Central to the in-service training of teachers is the support and encouragement of administrative officials, whether in national Ministries of Education or on local school boards, depending upon the organization of the nation's school system. If these officials make it clear they are interested in teaching about the United Nations in the schools they control, teachers who want to conduct such teaching feel free to do so and those who have been reluctant or afraid to carry it out are more likely to attempt it.

Since most nations have centralized school systems, it is officials in the Ministry of Education who must take the initiative in promoting the study of the United Nations and its related agencies. The initial step is usually the issuing of a statement or directive by them. A typical one is included in the Official Curriculum for Elementary Schools in Sweden. It says: 'In teaching of international affairs, attention should be directed primarily to the United Nations, including the content and implications of the Universal Declaration of Human Rights.' Specific mention is made of Unesco and the World Health Organization and it is recommended that special stress be laid on fields in which co-operation has been effective.

Such directives are imperative in many countries and extremely useful in others. But they need implementation. Too often governments issue general statements and then fail to follow them through with action.

Another step which has been taken in a few cases is to provide special teachers who travel round the country teaching about the United Nations system in a large number of schools and serving as consultants on this subject. The report from Liberia refers to such a 'travelling teacher' for two areas in that country and the Swedish report mentions that the National Commission for Unesco and the United Nations Association have jointly sponsored the appointment of a consultant to assist with programmes on the United Nations system and in education for international understanding in Sweden. The Italian report states that in order to widen its area of operations the Italian Society for International

Organization has organized lecture tours since 1958 in co-operation with local school authorities. The report recognizes the limitations of such a programme, however, pointing out that to be truly effective, the number of lectures delivered on such tours should be increased many times. A reference is made to the use of filmstrips on the United Nations system as one of the most effective methods applied in these lectures.

A unique situation exists in the United States where a full time 'observer' is employed by the National Education Association to follow the varied activities of the United Nations system and inform the many members of this teachers' organization of current happenings of interest to them. The report from India refers to the many people who have participated in the activities of the United Nations and its specialized agencies as a source of competent speakers for school and in-service programme. They are often very busy and cannot always give the time to speak to groups of school children or teachers, but there are some who are able to do this. Men and women now engaged in United Nations activities could also be invited from time to time to meet teachers' groups. Requests for their services, however, should be limited in number and confined in most instances to fairly large groups of teachers so that the time spent may be used most profitably.

It is often wise to encourage teachers to develop specialties within the curriculum. This is especially true of primary grade teachers. Because they are required to teach so many different subjects they are often unable to explore any one field or specialty in depth. School officials might find it helpful to encourage a limited number of teachers to develop the subject of teaching about the United Nations and its agencies as a special field of competence. This can be done by channelling articles and brochures to them for reading and review, asking them to report to other teachers on their reactions to these materials, sending them to conferences and seminars and in some cases giving them time to prepare and try out special materials on the United Nations system in their classes. The imaginative teacher is not likely to need suggested units of study or model lesson plans on the United Nations. But there are thousands of busy teachers with little experience in this field who could profit from ideas passed on by individuals with a

creative flair. Some school systems ask a few individuals to prepare
examples of lesson plans and units for use by many teachers.

The Indian Government, in conjunction with the Office of Public
Information of the United Nations, has prepared a series of lesson
plans on the United Nations family to be distributed widely in
that nation as an aid to in-service teachers. The French National
Educational Institute has published a book of lessons which has
been much used, called *Leçons sur les Nations Unies et les Institutions Spécialisées*. In the United States many city and state school
systems have issued 'resource units' for teachers on teaching
about the United Nations. These are compendia of background
material, ideas for lessons and annotated bibliographies of a wide
variety of resources for use by teachers and students. From them
classroom teachers can select the materials and ideas which they
deem appropriate for their work. Some of them were prepared by
classroom teachers working as a group and some by curriculum
bureaux in city or state systems.

United Nations publications of special value to teachers, and
their sources, are listed under the sub-heading 'In Teacher-training
Institutions' of this chapter, and under the sub-heading 'Textbooks and Supplementary Reading Materials' in Chapter 6.

A most useful document for teachers all over the world would
be a film or a filmstrip telling the story of the study of the United
Nations system by a class at almost any grade level over a period
of two or three weeks.[1] This might be prepared without captions
so that it could be used in many countries with a script in different
languages. An individual school, a school system or a teachers'
college might well pioneer in this way and thus help thousands of
teachers in all parts of the globe. Even the preparation of lists of
materials on the United Nations system and the places from which
they can be obtained would be a useful in-service project. There
should certainly be such a list in every Member State of the United
Nations and its agencies, prepared locally, so that not only United
Nations publications but all the materials available in that nation

---

1. The Japanese National Commission for Unesco has published a filmstrip,
in colour, illustrating the various activities, in and out of the classroom,
used in participating in the Unesco Associated Schools Project.

would be included. This has been done already in many countries by the Ministry of Education, a teachers' organization or the national branch of the United Nations Association.

Perhaps the method which has produced the best results to date in the in-service education of teachers is the seminar. It is mentioned many times in the 1960 report. Among those making specific references to seminars are Austria, Brazil, Burma, the Federal Republic of Germany, Greece, India, Italy, Japan, Norway, Sweden, the United Kingdom and the United States of America. In previous reports many other nations have mentioned the value of these meetings of teachers. Such seminars are held for periods ranging from two days to two or more weeks. During this time a wide variety of activities is offered, including lectures, films, discussions, demonstration lessons, and exhibitions. Often for part of the time, the participants divide into working groups organized by grade levels or topics, to discuss common problems and prepare materials for use by other teachers. Seminars usually begin with a key address by an outside speaker or with a film, giving the participants a common experience before they form into groups. Living in a community, sharing in social activities and having some time for informal conversations enhances the value of the participants' experience.

Seminars are run by different organizations in different countries. The 1960 report mentions seminars held by Unesco National Commissions, teachers' groups, Ministries of Education or school systems and by non-governmental organizations such as the United Nations Associations. Unesco has continued to support seminars for teachers, usually giving financial assistance to National Commissions or non-governmental organizations, rather than conducting such conferences directly. For example, since 1955, the Unesco Institute of Education (Hamburg), in collaboration with the respective National Commissions and with assistance from Unesco, has organized seminars in Austria, Czechoslovakia, France, Germany, Italy, Norway and Turkey. Each meeting was attended by about thirty-five participants from up to nineteen different countries.

Since 1949 the World Federation of United Nations Associations has held nineteen regional seminars with aid in most instances from Unesco. In recent years these meetings have taken place in Australia, Denmark, the Federal Republic of Germany, Ghana, Italy and Pakistan. One of the most interesting publications to be issued as a result of these seminars is the teachers' guide *L'Enseignement sur la Famille des Nations Unies*,[1] published by WFUNA following the seminar for teachers in Italy in 1957.

Two large-scale seminars on teaching about the United Nations were held in Greece in 1957 and in 1959, sponsored by the United Nations and its Information Centre in Athens. A similar meeting was organized in Ankara, Turkey, in 1960.

These are a few of the ways in which in-service training of teachers can be carried out with profit to all. Many other ways not mentioned here have been devised. Taken together they have had a powerful impact on the training of teachers in education on the United Nations family. It is hoped that this will increase in the near future and that even more teachers will be reached and helped.

Through out-of-school organizations

There are millions of people in the world who will never be reached in schools. Their opinions count, directly or indirectly, in shaping national and world opinion no matter what form of government they live under. Many of them know a little about the United Nations and its agencies but their information is often limited and frequently incorrect.

If they are to learn about the United Nations system it must be through out-of-school activities and institutions. These may vary from country to country but newspapers, public gatherings and entertainments and stores or markets are to be found in most communities. The people must be reached where they ordinarily meet, which may be in the evening in a large market after most of the trading for the day is done, or in gatherings of young people, farmers or labourers. It is also important to approach them in ways that are likely to appeal. Farmers may be most interested

1. *L'Enseignement sur la Famille des Nations Unies dans les Pays de la Région de la Méditerranée du Nord*, Geneva, WFUNA, 1959.

in a demonstration of a new way to grow rice or in a film showing how, with the help of the Food and Agriculture Organization, other farmers improved the yield of their crops. Mothers may be interested in how United Nations organizations have helped to develop health clinics and maternity centres or how the women of a particular country gained the right to vote. Young people may be interested in the Work Camp movement which Unesco has encouraged or in opportunities to study abroad which are publicized by Unesco. This may sound very obvious but all too often educational programmes about the United Nations seem meaningless to the people to whom they are presented.

Many governments have assumed a major share of the responsibility for informing their citizens, but some responsibility lies with the United Nations and its agencies. There are forty-three Information Centres throughout the world including the information offices attached to each of the regional economic commissions. Through publications, radio and television programmes, films and filmstrips, and through co-operative efforts with national information agencies, the United Nations and its agencies reach millions of people. Many publications are printed in several languages and assistance is given to governments to adapt and publish them in others. *The Universal Declaration of Human Rights,* for example, has now appeared in sixty languages. An increasing proportion of the publications budget has been made available to Information Centres for local production, adaptation, and initiation of publications: $75,000 in 1959 as compared with $50,000 in 1958. The production of films and filmstrips has continued and many governments and organizations have been helped in preparing similar visual aids on a wide variety of topics. One of the United Nations most important services is the information it gives to press and radio services reaching millions of people daily. Its Office of Public Information has held a number of conferences attended by representatives of as many as 200 non-governmental organizations. During the period 1956 to 1959, meetings were held in Havana, Santiago de Chile, Rome, Buenos Aires, Bogotá and at United Nations headquarters in New York City.

Programmes of public information are also carried out by the specialized agencies. Typical of their work, and of primary concern to readers of this book, are the activities of Unesco. Some idea of the extent of its publications programme may be gathered from the fact that between 1956 and 1960 it distributed 3.5 million items, such as display sheets, poster sets, manuals, booklets and reprints from magazines, on its aims and activities. National Commissions for Unesco and national non-governmental organizations have been encouraged and helped to produce their own language versions of these materials which have appeared in twenty-five languages other than English, French and Spanish. *The Unesco Courier*, a monthly illustrated magazine, is printed in Arabic, English, French, Italian, Japanese, German, Spanish and Russian, and has a circulation of over 200,000. In radio, during this same period, more than 20,000 recordings of interviews, discussions, weekly commentaries and feature programmes were distributed in twenty-three languages. A series of half-hour programmes, called 'Easy as A-B-C', on the aims and work of Unesco, produced in conjunction with the Radio Division of the United Nations, has been a particular success. Unesco has also produced films, filmstrips and travelling exhibitions on cultural and scientific themes.

In addition to organizing seminars and conferences for teachers (see under 'Through Help to Teachers in Service' above), Unesco gives financial and technical assistance to seminars for leaders of adult and youth education at which the work of the United Nations and its agencies is discussed. It co-operates closely with federations of Unesco clubs in France and the Federal Republic of Germany and has set up a system of Associated Youth Projects, whereby advice and assistance are given to youth groups undertaking approved projects to develop international understanding.

One way to enlist the support of many out-of-school agencies is by celebrating special days and weeks such as United Nations Day and Week, Human Rights Day and Week and World Health Day and Week. Most groups in a community can take part in these celebrations by appearing in parades, offering their store windows or aisles for exhibits, showing films on the United Nations in the local theatre or helping to organize a festival or fair featuring the United Nations and its agencies. In a few countries United

Nations trees have been planted with appropriate ceremonies and families encouraged to have special United Nations meals. The press and radio are usually willing to co-operate in such activities. By these means people are given information and there are often emotional overtones as well, both helpful in engendering support for the United Nations.

But programmes should not be limited to annual events. People and organizations interested in enlightening the public on the progress and problems of the United Nations system should try to arrange for local newspapers and radio and television stations to provide regular up-to-date and accurate accounts of United Nations activities. This is especially important in countries where few people read newspapers. Films, too, are likely to reach far greater audiences than the printed word. Many governments have used mobile film units as a special medium for mass education. They might be encouraged to show some of the United Nations outstanding films in their programmes, especially in areas which are comparatively isolated from other sources of news. As new nations develop their national television systems, this medium can be increasingly used.

The public library is an important educational institution, and films, exhibitions and lectures are often included in its services. The United States' contribution to the 1960 report devotes a large section to 'The Public Library: A Community Resource on the United Nations.' There are also travelling libraries or 'bookmobiles', special trucks equipped for use in outlying districts where people do not have easy access to ordinary libraries. The potentialities of this community institution should not be overlooked. Local libraries should have at least a minimum collection of books and pamphlets on the United Nations and its agencies as well as such magazines as *The Unesco Courier* and the *United Nations Review*.

In most countries out-of-school education is provided mainly through the efforts of voluntary non-governmental bodies, representing many different interests and activities, professional, cultural, educational, scientific and humanistic. These associations assist schools by providing speakers and teaching materials and stimulate and collaborate in celebrations of special days in the

United Nations calendar. In the 1960 report Austria, China, Italy, the United Kingdom, the United States and other countries refer to the work of the United Nations Associations in promoting understanding of the United Nations, both in schools and through out-of-school activities, and to the important contribution of youth groups affiliated to them.

The World Federation of United Nations Associations, which groups national branches in fifty countries,[1] was established to promote support for the United Nations and to spread information about its aims and activities. Mention has already been made of WFUNA's work in school education and teacher training on the regional and national scale. In addition national United Nations Associations, through their local branches and often in co-operation with local groups—trade unions, women's guilds, youth clubs, etc.—organize public meetings, film shows, brain trusts, debates and other activities. The United Nations Associations generally publish their own journals or news-sheets and help to distribute United Nations publications. They have been closely involved in practical aid projects ; World Refugee Year, for example, and the Freedom from Hunger Campaign, which have made a strong impact on public opinion.

Youth groups such as Boy Scouts, Girl Scouts and Girl Guides are active in many countries. These and similar organizations have included work on the United Nations family in their general programmes. They might be encouraged to do more. Out-of-school clubs can also serve as centres for this teaching. In the 1960 report the U.S.S.R. mentioned that political information sessions held in student clubs outside school hours constituted an important part of the programme for Soviet youth. Many of the United Nations Associations have youth groups affiliated to their national organizations reaching a large number of young people outside the schools.

One of the most ambitious and extensive programmes for youth is carried out by the Council for Education in World Citizenship in the United Kingdom, an affiliate of the national United Nations Association. The 1960 report has a full description of this

1. See Appendix 5 for addresses of national United Nations Associations.

organization which works both in and out of schools. During the 1956-59 period the CEWC held 180 conferences, including its wellknown Christmas Holiday Lectures in London, furnished 1,000 speakers, issued 2,900 visual aids to schools and youth organizations, ran an overseas correspondence service linking approximately 6,000 children with pen-friends in forty-two countries, produced seven issues yearly of a current affairs newspaper specially emphasizing the United Nations system, held conferences for teachers and youth workers, and distributed a monthly 'News Letter' (accompanied by the latest United Nations pamphlets) and 'Information Notes' for teachers.

The museum is another community institution which can help as an educational centre by organizing exhibitions on the work of the United Nations and its specialized agencies and on the cultural, social and economic characteristics of their Member States.

These are some of the ways to reach the very large number of people not in school. Every effort should be made to interest this tremendous population in the story of the work of the United Nations and interpret it to them in terms they can understand and appreciate.

6 General methods and resources for teaching about the United Nations and its related agencies

In any teaching there are many possible methods and a wide variety of resources. This is as true of teaching about the United Nations as it is of other topics. In this chapter we shall examine some of these methods and some of the resources available. As they dovetail so well, they are treated together following some introductory remarks about each individually. In this way it is hoped that their close relationship in teaching will be brought out and that readers will be saved the cross-referring which would otherwise be necessary.

Criteria for selecting the methods to be used

Many different methods are suggested here and one may well ask how to choose amongst them. The writer considers there are at least five criteria.

One is the aim to be achieved. For example, if a teacher wants to arouse interest in the United Nations and its agencies, a film or a group of pictures may be the best possible method. If he wants students to develop a fairly deep understanding of a problem with which the United Nations deals, a variety of documents, books and clippings would be best. A second is the needs of the members of a class. If they need to learn some of the skills involved in elementary research then individual research papers on some theme or topic concerning the United Nations system should be selected as the method. If, however, the group needs to develop an understanding of how people of another nation feel about a given problem, then acting and dramatics is more likely to produce the desired results.

A third is the teacher's own 'style'. Different teachers are successful with different methods. One may be able to use choral speaking as a device for arousing interest in the United Nations system and for developing background information whereas another may be especially apt in the use of debates and panel discussions. Each teacher should develop his or her own method or style, not forgetting to try a new method occasionally to acquire new, and often more effective, teaching techniques. A fourth is the availability of resources. Some of the methods suggested here will have to be eliminated because of the impossibility of obtaining films and filmstrips or adequate research materials with which to work. The fifth criterion is variety. For students who have used textbooks day after day, week in and week out, the introduction of a panel discussion (with proper preparation) can add excitement and enhance the possibilities of learning, or the introduction of pictures and posters or films and filmstrips may lift the level of learning because of the interest aroused by a novel approach.

It is hoped that teachers will find many old favourites among the methods mentioned in this chapter and some new approaches which they will want to attempt.

Comments on the resources for teaching about the United Nations system

In the last few years a great deal of work has gone into preparing materials on the United Nations. Some has been done by the United Nations and its agencies, some by governments and non-governmental organizations and some by school systems and individuals. Much time and effort have been expended and results have been encouraging. There is a wealth of material of many kinds now available on the United Nations system. Some of it is highly original in approach, well written and well produced. A few items are even exciting, like the remarkable ten-minute film produced by the United Nations called *Overture,* in which the music and pictures carry the story powerfully without any speaking.

However, it is clear that there are still large gaps. Most materials are in English or French, with occasional publications in other languages, in spite of the determined efforts of many people to produce more in other languages. Large pictures and posters are often very effective but they are difficult and costly to obtain. Sets of very large pictures, preferably mounted on cardboard, could be among the most useful resources for teachers everywhere and especially for those without film and filmstrip equipment.

There is a growing volume of literature for secondary school students but as yet very few books or booklets for children in the primary grades.

Although there has been progress, the paucity of materials is still a great problem. This was emphasized in the 1960 report which stated: 'The broad conclusion that emerges from the available evidence is that, while there has been some progress, the supply of teaching material still remains inadequate in one way or another in all countries.'

The report points out that while the United Nations and specialized agencies can do something to improve this situation, the major responsibility must be assumed by national governments.

To obtain materials which exist at present, teachers should bear in mind the major sources of information. They vary from country to country but in general they are as follows:

1. United Nations Information Centres.[1]
2. National Ministries of Education or other administrative bodies for schools.
3. National teachers' organizations.
4. National Commissions for Unesco.
5. Headquarters and Information Offices of specialized agencies in some countries.[1]

1. The addresses of these are given in Appendix 5. See the same Appendix for addresses of Unesco depository libraries.

6. National branches of the World Federation of United Nations Associations.[1]
7. National or local branches of other non-governmental organizations.

One service any government or non-governmental organization could perform is to publish a brief list of all materials now available in its country with the necessary addresses for obtaining them. This has been done in some countries but certainly not in all. A few schools could be designated as information centres with curriculum laboratories or resource centres established in them, until such time as all schools are better equipped.

Some teachers, glancing at the table of contents of this booklet or running through the headings in this chapter, may have come to the conclusion that teaching about the United Nations and its agencies can be carried out only in schools which are well equipped and staffed by highly-trained teachers. Many suggestions assume the existence of resources some schools may not have. But a careful examination of the ideas in the following pages should reveal that they can often be used in schools not rich in resources or by teachers not yet proficient in various methods of instruction.

The teacher in a rural school in an economically underdeveloped country, for example, may have only a room with four walls and a dirt floor assigned to him as a classroom. But blackboards can be improvised with a few pieces of wood and some black paint and walls can be used for maps, charts and drawings even if the teacher and students must resort to the use of charred sticks, soft shale rock or paint to make them. News clippings and pictures can be obtained from newspapers and magazines collected in the community. Radios have become fairly common in most parts of the world and if a school does not have its own, students can sometimes listen to broadcasts in the village square or compound or the home of a local resident. Pupils can co-operate in tracing outline maps on the ground in the school yard, learning as they work. Simple plays can be written and acted with a minimum of improvised

---

1. The addresses of these are given in Appendix 5. See the same appendix for addresses of Unesco depository libraries.

stage properties and role-playing and choral speaking can be developed.

In ways like these the teacher whose classroom is bare at the beginning of term, may be able to use or adapt some of the suggestions given below for supplementary teaching methods and resources. His is a difficult task but not a hopeless one. Some of the most ingenious and creative teaching this writer has seen was in schools of this type in many parts of the world and some of the most prosaic and unimaginative was in schools that were elaborately and expensively equipped. Resources are extremely useful but they do not guarantee good teaching.

With these considerations regarding methods and resources in mind, let us turn to more specific suggestions on ways and means of teaching about the United Nations and its related agencies.

*Textbooks and supplementary
reading materials*

Among a wide variety of methods and materials, reading is the principal method and books the basic materials for learning about the United Nations system.

With young children most of this teaching should be by means of stories told by the teacher and through pictorial methods but reading materials should be used even in the first three or four years at school. Some of these should be selected for the teacher to read aloud, and others for the children themselves to read. Although few in number such books do exist. A popular printed account is the book *A Garden We Planted Together*,[1] published in co-operation with the United Nations with pictures from the United Nations filmstrip of the same title. This brief allegory, which has been translated into several languages, tells the story of a children's garden in which some plants grew and others died until the children decided to work together to dig ditches to provide water for all parts of the garden. At the end the garden is likened to the United Nations. *Three Promises to You*,[2] a picture

1. *A Garden We Planted Together*, New York, McGraw-Hill, 1952, 48 p.
2. Munro Leaf, *Three Promises to You*, Philadelphia, Lippincott, in co-operation with the United Nations Department of Public Information, 1957.

book for children aged 6 to 10 on the aims and work of the United Nations, is adapted from the United Nations filmstrip of that name.

Special accounts for upper primary and secondary school students are fortunately more numerous. This is understandable since so much more can be taught in these grades. In the 1960 report, textbooks and supplementary materials on the United Nations were listed for many countries while others mentioned that they were preparing texts. Among these were Iceland, Israel, and Yugoslavia. At the eleventh Regional Conference of Non-Governmental Organizations in Bogota in 1959 a resolution was passed inviting Colombia, Ecuador, Peru and Venezuela to prepare and distribute a textbook on the subject. This is an excellent example of co-operation among nations to foster teaching about the United Nations family. Several countries stated in the 1960 report that chapters on the United Nations are included in school textbooks, for example, in Austria, Iran, Switzerland and the U.A.R.

Especially published weekly or monthly current events papers are a form of supplementary reading used with success in some countries for pupils in upper primary and middle grades as well as more advanced students.

Wide use is made with this age-group of magazines like *The Unesco Courier*, the *United Nations Review*, *World Health*, *The ILO News* and any illustrated publication or picture sheets which may be available. Other supplementary materials mentioned in the 1960 report include: bulletins, instructions, circulars, sample lessons and pamphlet material issued by educational authorities; films, filmstrips, posters and recordings; discussion guides for teachers and pupils; background information and teaching suggestions in professional journals for teachers; materials for school exhibitions.

Some of these are discussed in later sections of this chapter.

To provide more reading material on the United Nations for students, several countries have translated books and pamphlets into their own languages, sometimes with assistance from the United Nations or from Unesco. In addition to textbooks and supplementary material secondary school students can use some of the more detailed information material on the United Nations and its related agencies. Almost all students should be familiar with at least some part of the Charter of the United Nations as the basic document of the organization, and of the Universal Declaration of Human Rights. These are now available in many different languages.

For introductory reading most secondary school students can use the series of leaflets on each of the main bodies of the United Nations and the specialized agencies, called '. . . , What it is . . . , What it does . . . , How it works . . .'. These have eight to fourteen pages and are available in several languages. A great many students at this level can also read with profit many of the articles in the *United Nations Review*, published monthly in English, French and Spanish versions. The review often deals with special topics and each October includes an article on the issues to be discussed at the forthcoming General Assembly. Each number contains a survey of news for the month and a digest of all United Nations decisions with documentary references to make this record as complete as possible. The November or December number always covers the debates in the General Assembly and includes some verbatim reports. Often articles from this journal are reprinted for wider distribution like the pamphlet published in 1961 called *The United Nations and the Status of Women*.

A useful document for students and teachers is the booklet *Basic Facts about the United Nations*, a small pamphlet dealing with the aims, organization, and activities of all parts of the United Nations system as well as their interrelationships. It is issued in several languages and is frequently revised to keep the information it provides up to date. The present edition (1962) is the seventeenth.

The United Nations Family and *United Nations Work and Structure* are two pamphlets published by the United Nations for free distribution that give a clear and comprehensive account of the organization, its various bodies and related agencies and their separate functions and aims.

Other useful publications are *For Human Welfare* (a guide to the work of the Economic and Social Council), *Co-operation for Economic Progress* (on the work of the four regional Economic

Commissions), *Technical Assistance* (on the international aid administered by the United Nations), two booklets on problems of human rights, *A Standard of Achievement* and *United Nations Work for Human Rights*, and the recently published *Guide to the Charter of the United Nations* which traces the history of the founding of the United Nations and explains how the structure of the organization is planned to interpret the terms of the Charter.

There are a number of authoritative accounts of the work of the United Nations published annually, or regularly brought up to date. These provide valuable reference material and are useful sources for research by teachers, lecturers, textbook writers, university students and, to a lesser extent, advanced secondary school students. For example, most secondary school students should be able to use the *Annual Report of the Secretary-General* and especially its *Introduction* issued separately. Mature students in secondary schools and older people will find *Everyman's United Nations* and the *Yearbook of the United Nations* mines of useful data on almost all aspects of the United Nations system. *Everyman's United Nations* (6th edition, 1959) is a compact reference book summarizing the work of the United Nations family from 1945 to 1958 and giving its history. *The Yearbook of the United Nations* has been issued annually since 1947. Part I deals with the debates in the General Assembly and Part II with the activities of other sections of the United Nations system. There are also periodical studies such as the annual *World Economic Survey* and the biennial *Report on the World Social Situation* published by the United Nations.[1]

These and other helpful documents can be obtained on loan from many libraries, purchased from sales agents of the United Nations or Unesco in various parts of the world or consulted in the reading rooms of United Nations Information Centres.[2]

Articles in newspapers and magazines are useful material. Occasionally these are by outstanding authorities on the United Nations and should be clipped and saved for future reference.

1. See also *World Facts and Figures*, New York, United Nations, 40 p. $0.25, 1/6 (stg.), 1 Sw.Fr. (United Nations sales No. 62.I.4.)
2. See Appendix 5.

*Current events and current events
papers*

In some countries considerable emphasis is placed on the study
of current events and contemporary affairs. It is hoped that
students will thus become interested in local, national and international events, that they will form the habit of keeping up with
the news, and that what they learn from their textbooks will be
enriched and brought up to date.

This approach has great value. Students can follow the daily
progress of the United Nations, especially during sessions of the
General Assembly, and their interest in its activities should be
increased. But there are risks. One is that the coverage may be
superficial and another that students will be confronted only with
the explosive issues aired in the General Assembly. These can be
avoided if teachers arrange for longer periods on a few topics
dealing with the United Nations rather than try to cover a wide
variety, and if they ensure that other aspects of the United Nations
system are discussed as well as the General Assembly and Security
Council. One way to develop depth is to ask various students to
become 'experts' for a few weeks on a particular issue or the role
of a country in the United Nations, reporting their findings to
the class from time to time.

In this approach much use is made of daily newspapers and
radio and television broadcasts. In some countries there are special
weekly newspapers for children. In the 1960 report Canada,
Norway and the United States referred to such publications and
they exist in other countries too. Teachers and librarians should
keep these as supplementary material for future use by other
students.

Pictures, posters, charts and cartoons

Pictures are very valuable materials for teaching and an extremely
fine method of instruction. Often a picture can tell a story more
vividly than words. To someone who has never seen yaws or
leprosy, pictures are more striking. A series of photographs is
the best way to show what life is like in an Arab refugee camp in
the Gaza Strip. To know what the brightly-coloured *kente* cloth

robes of West Africans look like, a picture provides an accurate answer.

Pictures relating to the work of the United Nations can be collected from newspapers and magazines. Especially valuable sources are the illustrated news magazines now so popular in many parts of the world. Occasionally posters are available from the United Nations Information Centres but no titles are mentioned here as their supplies are quickly exhausted and the same sets of posters are seldom reprinted. Such magazines as *The Unesco Courier, World Health,* and the *United Nations Review* are likewise excellent sources for pictorial materials, including charts.

The best way to use pictures, posters and charts is to mount them on cardboard and show them with an opaque projector which enlarges them so that the whole class can see them. Where this is impossible the teacher should move from group to group or row to row exhibiting the pictorial materials; or they can be passed from pupil to pupil. Such materials, however, should be studied rather than just looked at. It is often amazing what students will observe if they are asked: 'What do you see?' Six or seven pictures may be sufficient to provoke a discussion of forty or fifty minutes when this is done.

Cartoons are more difficult to obtain but they appear in some newspapers and magazines. Often they depict ideas that are very difficult to express succinctly in words. The cartoon is frequently considered a rather simple method of expressing ideas. In fact they are generally very subtle and are appreciated only by the more sophisticated. Teachers and educators would do well to collect cartoons as excellent teaching aids.

There is a great need for pictures, posters, charts and photo sheets for use in schools and in adult education groups. Although expensive to produce the results are almost always worth the outlay. A few series of posters, mounted on cardboard with eyelets so that they can be hung in classrooms, would be an extremely useful publishing project for any government, school system, non-governmental organization or the United Nations itself. Perhaps a review of the place of such pictorial materials in teaching about the United Nations and its related agencies could be undertaken by groups interested in this topic.

*Flannelboards, wall newspapers,
bulletin boards and exhibits*

The flannelboard is not widely used but can be vivid and effective, especially in portraying the structure of the United Nations organization. A large piece of wood or cardboard is covered with flannel with a thick nap, preferably grey or black. Then cardboard or heavy paper discs are cut out and flannel pasted on their backs. These are used to represent the various organs of the United Nations and the specialized agencies. They are placed on the flannelboard as they are discussed until the entire United Nations system is assembled. The same material can be presented on a blackboard or on large sheets of paper but the flannelboard diagram has the advantage of colour and movement and of being constructed at the pace of the work in progress.

This device can be used, of course, for other work such as bar graphs on the United Nations income and expenses or the *per capita* income of various Member States, pictures of the work of some of the specialized agencies or of outstanding personalities connected with these organizations.

Wall newspapers are an especially good teaching device in countries where a large number of persons do not read and where newspapers are rare. They can be effective pictorial accounts and should be displayed so as to reach the widest possible audience.

Bulletin boards are fairly common in schools in most countries but should also be used in factories, stores, libraries and public buildings.

Large exhibits are expensive and difficult to transport but are seen by thousands of people and have great eye appeal. Less ambitious exhibitions can be arranged by schools and organizations in any community. The Belgian statement in the 1960 report refers specifically to exhibitions, stating that 'circulating expositions dealing with the United Nations, Unesco, human rights, the Near and Far East, and the mutual appreciation of Eastern and Western cultural values, travel from city to city and village to village'.

Films and filmstrips

Few teaching methods are more effective than films and filmstrips. Both are of value and both have weaknesses.

Films can give everyone a front seat at major meetings of the United Nations and its agencies or an armchair view of places all over the world where United Nations representatives are working. The events of months or even years can be telescoped into a few minutes on film and sound and colour added to heighten the reality. But films have their drawbacks. They may not be fully comprehended unless followed by discussion, and of course there are innumerable places where projectors are not available. In some ways filmstrips are superior to films, at least for school use. They are less expensive and easier to operate. A filmstrip can be interrupted for discussion or turned back to clarify or underline a point.

Since its inception the United Nations has produced more than a hundred films and the specialized agencies many more. It is difficult to supply sound tracks in all the required languages but the United Nations has done much in this respect. In 1960, for example, it produced a special *UN Trailer* with the sound track in thirty-six languages, its most ambitious undertaking so far. A good many of its recent films have appeared in Chinese, English, French, Indonesian, Norwegian, Persian, Portuguese, Spanish, Thai and Urdu. Films of special interest to particular countries have been produced in the appropriate languages.

It is difficult to single out just a few films of widespread interest but a short list could include the new, short documentary series on *The United Nations Charter* ; *The General Assembly* ; *The Security Council* ; and *The Trusteeship Council*, with others on the specialized agencies to follow. *Workshop for Peace*, a thirty-minute film of a complete tour of United Nations headquarters, has been a great success, as also the ten-minute film *Overture*, mentioned earlier. A film produced in 1961 with the title *Half of Mankind* tells the story of the Technical Assistance programme in non-industrial countries and promises to be very popular. For children, the films *Danish Children Build a Greek School* ; *Three of Our Children* (on the work of Unicef in Europe, Africa and the Far

East) ; and *Assignment Children* (an account of Danny Kaye's trip round the world for Unicef) have been successful.

In the 1960 report it was pointed out that in addition to the films it has produced, Unesco has contributed to the production costs of *A Fable for Friendship*, a colour cartoon on the aims of the United Nations drawn by the famous Czech artist Jiri Trnka, and a film on fundamental education at Sartano in Southern Italy produced by a Danish firm. In recent years Australia has produced two films on the United Nations: *Across the Frontiers*, a film for secondary schools on the aims and work of Unesco with special reference to Australia and South Asia, and *Born Equal*, a film for upper elementary and secondary schools on the Universal Declaration of Human Rights.

The United Nations and its agencies have produced a number of filmstrips, among them two for young children: *A Garden We Planted Together* and *Three Promises*. For secondary school students typical titles are *Structure for Peace; How the United Nations Works; The General Assembly of the United Nations; United Nations: Blueprint for Peace; Towards a Better World: How the United Nations Began; For Social Progress* and *For Economic Progress* (on the work of the Economic and Social Council) ; *Progress through Sharing Skills* (on the activities of the specialized agencies) ; *Let There Be Life* (on WHO and Unicef); *Let There Be Bread* (on the work of FAO) ; and *To Combine Their Efforts* (on United Nations permanent headquarters). Filmstrips produced by Unesco rencetly have stressed major Unesco projects and include *Water in the Arid Zones; Clouds and Meteors; Source of Happiness;* and *The UN in Asia.*

Australia and Uruguay amongst others have produced filmstrips for use in their schools. Australia has a twenty-four frame filmstrip called *Ten Years Towards Peace* and Uruguay a series of filmstrips to accompany twenty-five lectures on the United Nations system. The Australian Teachers' Federation has printed a filmstrip on *The United Nations: Towards a Better World* and the Danish Laererforening has one on *Suez* describing the United Nations' efforts in that crisis. Both of these were made as part of a project organized by the World Confederation of Organizations of the Teaching Profession, with assistance from Unesco.

Radio, recordings and tape
recordings and television

Radio is a very common means of communication today and its potential in telling the story of the United Nations system is tremendous.

The United Nations Radio Division devotes most of its time to the preparation of fifteen-minute weekly broadcasts which in 1959, for example, were given in thirty-one languages in more than ninety countries. It distributed about 25,000 discs or tapes between 1956 and 1959 to stations all over the world. It has also provided news reports in twenty-nine languages broadcast by fifty-five radio stations in Member States. It co-operates with radio divisions of national, regional and community Departments of Education.

Unesco has carried on very similar activities in radio, distributing in the 1956 to 1959 period more than 20,000 recordings in twenty-three languages to ninety-eight countries. In 1957 it produced a special series of thirty programmes in ten languages on the International Atomic Energy Agency and in 1959 another forty-four such programmes in nine languages. It distributed tapes or scripts of some sixty programmes for use in teaching on the United Nations family.

The 1960 report includes a report from Australia on the use of radio. This mentions the introduction in 1958 of a series of twelve programmes on 'The Family of Mankind' produced by the Australian Broadcasting Company in co-operation with the State Directors of Education, as well as several other programmes. New Zealand referred briefly to the use of school radio programmes for the Tokelau Islands and the Norwegian Government reported on the use of the facilities of the Norwegian Broadcasting Company.

The educational possibilities of television are even greater in some ways than radio. Some use is already being made in education of this relatively new means of communication. At the time of the opening of the new Unesco headquarters in Paris in 1958 the French television network presented a programme 'Unesco en 2008', and a film of the inauguration ceremonies was sent to stations in thirty-five countries. Unesco's Major Project for Mutual

Appreciation of Eastern and Western Cultural Values has aroused considerable interest among television stations, with the French telecasting a series under the title 'Rendez-vous avec l'Orient' and the Federal Republic of Germany a round-table discussion on this theme. Thailand mentions the use of television programmes and in the United States a New York television channel has carried a UNTV series of thirty-minute programmes called 'Dateline United Nations', transmitted especially for school viewing.

Since educational radio and television will certainly expand enormously in the years ahead, these are two of the most powerful methods and resources for those interested in increasing and improving teaching about the United Nations and its related agencies.

Maps and map studies

Teachers everywhere are more aware of the use of maps than of many other methods mentioned in this chapter. It should suffice to point out that map-making with regard to the United Nations system should be used in every school. Since the United Nations and its agencies work in almost every part of the world, its study can be an important part of a course in geography.

Maps can be used in numerous ways—drawn on the floors of classrooms, on the walls or in the school grounds. Drawings made by pupils can be mounted on them.

For example, maps can be made showing projects financed by the International Bank, stations of the World Meteorological Organization, rice-producing nations assisted by the Food and Agriculture Organization or countries helped by Unicef and the World Health Organization to build plants for producing powdered milk.

Role-playing and plays

It is often difficult for students to imagine the thoughts and feelings of people of other countries. Yet little progress will be made in creating an international community unless people at least understand others' reactions even if they do not agree with them.

Students can learn to appreciate how others think and feel by playing the role of someone in another country or a representative of some other nation at a United Nations meeting or an official of the United Nations. The aim is to react as these people would in a given situation, 'stepping into their shoes' as it were. This teaching device is not yet widely used but is very highly recommended. A student of a country that has or has had colonies who wants to understand how people in a non-self-governing territory feel, will be more successful if he changes his name temporarily and assumes fully the role of someone desiring independence. To understand how citizens of another country feel about a vote in the United Nations one of the most effective methods is to play the role of a representative of that country and make the speech he might make to the General Assembly.

Acting plays is much more common in schools and other educational groups than role-playing. The United Nations Radio Division has produced a number of plays during the years of the United Nations' existence, but their scripts are not available to the general public. It would be extremely useful to have a collection of some of the best of these for use in schools, colleges and adult education groups.

Panel discussions and debates

These can be used successfully in classroom teaching or extra-curricular activities. They are particularly effective for presenting a variety of points of view on topics concerned with the United Nations system and its problems.

However, a word of caution is not out of place. They are of little use unless the participants have done considerable background reading, and in the case of debates the wording of the debate question must be clear and speakers' points of view for and against must be fairly well balanced.

Model assemblies

Model assemblies are being used increasingly in secondary schools, colleges and universities, and a variety of non-governmental organizations for the intensive study of specific problems. In schools these are usually carried out as extra-curricular activities involving representatives of several institutions. Their values are many and varied. They help participants to take a realistic view of the work of the United Nations and its agencies and encourage them to do a great deal of reading. They often result in the purchase of materials for school and college libraries. And they usually arouse considerable and, often, lasting interest among the audience as well.

Because of frequent inquiries about this type of teaching the Office of Public Information of the United Nations has prepared a publication, *How to Plan and Conduct Model UN Meetings*, at present available in English.[1]

It includes many hints for making model assemblies successful, suggesting, among other points, that they should:

1. Be long and carefully planned by a strong central steering committee.
2. Be sponsored by a school, school system or adult organization.
3. Enlist the active participation of at least one person familiar with the actual operation of the United Nations.
4. Make provision for adequate financing.
5. Be limited in scope to one part of the United Nations system, such as a meeting of the Security Council, the Economic and Social Council or the Unesco Executive Board.
6. Include adequate background reading materials for all participants.
7. Provide for the circulation, well in advance of the model assembly, of a provisional agenda.
8. Involve adequate preparation by the participants to present the views of the country or person they represent fairly, adequately and realistically.
9. Feature, wherever possible, at least one well-known and effective speaker to add depth and distinction to the proceedings.
10. Have a limited agenda with no surprises or hypothetical items.

1. *How to Plan and Conduct Model UN Meetings*, New York, Oceana Publications, 1961, 127 p.

11. Stress the selection of capable presiding officers.
12. Include printed rules of procedure.
13. Provide adequately for the housing and feeding of delegates coming from a distance.
14. Give attention, wherever possible, to follow-up activities, including the filing of all records of the meeting for use in the future.

One project the book recommends is a model meeting of Unesco's Executive Board, with its thirty members, highlighting one activity such as the extension of primary education in Latin America.

With sufficient time and resources a class or school can undertake a model assembly but this method lends itself best to a joint project involving several schools, colleges or adult groups.

In the 1960 report several nations mention the use of this method including Australia, Canada, Korea, the United Kingdom and the United States. The report from the United Kingdom refers to a variation of it used at a girls' high school where a 'Mock Trial' of Unesco was produced, and subsequently recorded by the Radio Division of Unesco.

Observances

The annual observance of United Nations Day on 24 October has become one of the most widespread means of teaching about the United Nations system. Reports from many countries mention special events on that day or for the entire week. Attention is also given in several countries to Human Rights Day on 10 December and to World Health Day on 7 April.

Such observances are of considerable value in schools and institutions of higher learning and even more so when they are community projects. Community activities are usually more colourful and elaborate than those conducted in schools and for children there is the added thrill of taking part in an adult event.

There is always a danger, however, that in a school or school system where one or more of these days is observed, it will be assumed that work on the United Nations has been completed for the year. In fact, the event should be regarded as part of a whole programme rather than the programme itself. Special days should either encourage further study or be the culmination of a long-term project on the United Nations family. It is always important to stress the participation of children and young people and not rely solely on a speech by a prominent adult on these occasions.

From time to time other special 'days' may be included in the calendar of special events. The report from the Philippines, for example, mentions national observance of ILO Day in 1959 in honour of that organization's fortieth anniversary and, also in that year, the celebration of National Health Week stressing the work of the World Health Organization. In the United States the autumn festival of Hallow-e'en has become the occasion for a very ambitious programme on the work of Unicef. Children in schools, church groups, youth clubs and other organizations learn about the work of Unicef and collect funds for it by door-to-door canvassing. In 1960 this special appeal brought in $1,750,000 for Unicef, much of it contributed by children.

Choral speaking

In some schools choral speaking is taught as part of language arts or speech courses. Students are divided into groups according to the pitch of their voices and learn to recite selected passages of literature either in antiphony or in unison. Speaking the Preamble to the Constitution of Unesco and the Preamble to the Charter of the United Nations in this manner has proved an effective teaching device. There are undoubtedly other United Nations documents that could be treated similarly.

Speeches and interviews

The use of outside speakers is another valuable practice. They are usually invited to lecture because of their past or present work with some part of the United Nations or one of its agencies or commissions. They can therefore speak with authority and, often, illustrate their talks with personal anecdotes while the novelty of having a new voice in a class, school assembly or club adds to the listeners' interest.

Some countries have appointed specialists on the United Nations system to travel from one school to another, showing films and filmstrips and speaking to several classes or an entire school at a time. Specialists have been used in Italy, Liberia and Sweden.

An alternative is for small groups of students to visit a United Nations expert or specialist on United Nations affairs in the locality and report on their conversation to the class or school. In some cases it might be possible to record the interviews on tape. As many students as possible should take part in the project by helping to frame questions to be asked at the interview, and so on. When interviews prove specially helpful, recordings or reports can be filed and used again later or loaned to other classes and schools.

Writing projects and contests

Children and young people can gain valuable experience in writing and composition and at the same time learn a great deal about the United Nations. In some schools pupils have made simplified versions of some of the basic documents of the organization and its agencies. Students have compiled scrapbooks with written comments on the work of various parts of the United Nations system or of the work of the United Nations in their own countries or larger geographical areas. Some have written biographies of outstanding men and women who have served the United Nations. Summaries of books and pamphlets on the United Nations have also been undertaken by many students. Far more ambitious projects can be attempted by college and university students including theses for degrees.

Among the most far-reaching programmes developed for students are the annual essay contests on the United Nations. These are often sponsored by local, regional and national divisions of United Nations Associations and thousands of students in many countries enter. Prizes are usually given for local and regional as well as national winners.

Elementary research on world problems and the use of yearly themes

Students should have some practice in elementary research during and after the secondary school period to acquire the skills needed for such work as well as much useful information. If students are allowed to select topics for themselves or from lists provided by teachers, their experience will be enhanced. The United Nations system embraces so many topics and countries that any student should be able to find a theme for intensive study. One intent on a medical training could discover what is being done about a major disease. A future farmer could study the work of the Food and Agriculture Organization in improving the yield of rice or in combating rinderpest. A future lawyer could explore some of the cases handled in recent years by the International Court of Justice, while the future teacher could do simple research on one of the many projects of Unesco.

Another method is to accent one general topic for a year or more. The most obvious choice would be one of the projects currently selected for emphasis by the United Nations for which special materials are available. Some school systems have followed this method, emphasizing the International Geophysical Year in 1957-58, World Refugee Year in 1959-60, and the present Freedom from Hunger Campaign[1] for the years from 1960 to 1965 and the United Nations Development Decade from 1960 to 1970.

When carrying out research, students should be reminded of the statement by Nasrollah Entezam, one-time President of the General Assembly, who said:

The work of the United Nations is just beginning. The world's problems are too many and too great to be solved in a single day, or in a year, or six years, or sixty. All your lives you, the youth of the world, will

1. See *Weather and Food*, Geneva, The World Meteorological Organization, 1962, 80 p., illus. This is the first in a series of Basic Studies supporting the Freedom from Hunger Campaign to be published by the FAO and other organizations of the United Nations. Subjects cover a wide range and include for example: population and food supplies; education and training in nutrition; animal diseases and human health; hunger and social policy; malnutrition and disease; economic development through food.

be hearing about collective security, human rights, technical assistance and the self-determination of nations. These are great ideas. Whether they flower into great civilizing forces or are lost in the footnotes of history will be up to you.

As a result of a research assignment a student may acquire a life-long interest in a particular subject or region.

United Nations work in different countries and regions

Students in the higher grades should know how the work of the United Nations and its agencies affects their country and the larger geographical region of which it is part. In this way they will realize the relevance of the United Nations in their lives and those of their friends and fellow countrymen and their study will take on a new significance. No study of the United Nations, however, should be entirely limited to one country or region.

This method is being used in several countries, as is indicated in recent reports to Unesco and the United Nations. Ghana refers to a new history syllabus for the sixth year in which one topic is 'Ghana and the United Nations'. In India post-graduate students have carried out research on 'The United Nations and Regional Organizations, with special reference to SEATO and NATO'. In Indonesia secondary school students make a special study of the relations between Indonesian independence and the United Nations.

A growing body of materials is available for such research. Reports of the economic commissions for various regions are excellent source material. National bodies interested in world affairs have published accounts of relations between their countries and the United Nations. Many United Nations publications are geared to this approach. For example, special issues of the WHO magazine *World Health* have been devoted to health problems in Africa, the Congo, Europe and South-East Asia, and the United Nations *Technical Assistance Newsletter* has had special issues on Africa, South-East Asia and other regions.

There are also a number of films and filmstrips dealing with particular countries or regions. Among them are *Help for Pakistan;*

Afghanistan Moves Ahead; Somaliland Votes; Indonesia Builds a Better Life; and *Ethiopia Advances.* Filmstrips include *Economic Developments in Africa; The Middle East and the United Nations;* and *Progress in South-East Asia.*

Specialized agencies and commissions

Quite young pupils can profitably study the work of the specialized agencies and commissions of the United Nations. In early years of school and the primary grades the emphasis could be on the work of Unicef, the Universal Postal Union, the Food and Agriculture Organization, the World Health Organization and some Unesco projects. Later, other specialized agencies and commissions can be introduced. The work of the United Nations Commission on the Status of Women might be stressed in classes for girls. The Commission on Human Rights is a very important part of the United Nations system; its activities and achievements can be studied at different age levels and from many angles.

History of the United Nations and using time lines

Students in all countries can learn about the foundation of the United Nations system and its forerunners as part of their history course. This could include some of the plans for international organizations mentioned in Chapter 2 and should certainly include some account of the development and decline of the League of Nations. Two difficulties in using this approach are that this topic is given little space in textbooks and that many students never reach the required point in their chronological study of history.

Where the historical background of the United Nations and its specialized agencies is studied, the use of a simple 'time line' is to be recommended as students can more easily grasp the time factor involved. The following is a highly simplified time line:

1920	1939-45	1945	1953	1960
Founding of the League of Nations	Second War World	Founding of the United Nations	Korean truce	Congo crisis

117

The line can be lengthened by adding as many items as desired, spacing them according to the time span involved.

People of the United Nations system

Reference has already been made in Chapter 2 to the biographical approach. This appeals to many young people and adults and should be widely used as a valuable means of learning. Unfortunately, biographical materials are not yet easily available. Much help could be given by the United Nations and its agencies, by governments, writers and publishers and non-governmental organizations.

Use of school and local libraries

The need for adequate school and local libraries should be apparent from the comments made in this booklet. Few schools and few communities have adequate libraries, let alone collections of material on the United Nations. Where libraries do exist, every encouragement should be given to those in charge to build up collections of books, booklets, pictorial materials, charts, posters and other useful documentation. School officials should investigate their present collections and give financial aid and encouragement to librarians to augment them. Non-governmental organizations and individuals could perform a useful service by assisting school and local libraries in this task.

In the meantime, teachers can pool their resources and make small collections of books, pamphlets, clippings and audio-visual materials. Kits or boxes of materials can sometimes be obtained for short periods on loan from larger libraries or local organizations. One of the finest services governments and non-governmental organizations could render in promoting teaching about the United Nations would be to prepare and distribute kits or boxes of materials to schools, youth clubs and adult education groups.

*Collecting illustrations and symbols
of the United Nations*

Fairly early in their life most children begin to make collections of some kind; postcards, dolls, stamps, coins or anything else arousing their interest or curiosity. This tendency can be put to good use. Children can be encouraged to collect United Nations postage stamps or flags of its Member States, or to keep scrapbooks of appropriate newscuttings and photographs. Mere collecting, however, teaches little. Some background reading and study is necessary to make any hobby meaningful. To encourage collectors the United Nations has produced a booklet on *United Nations Postage Stamps*[1] and a filmstrip called *Postmark: The Story of the United Nations Postage Stamps.*

One of the few symbols of the United Nations is the flag. Some schools fly it with their own national flag and others display it prominently at United Nations celebrations. There are many other ways of displaying its blue and white design, in poster work in art classes for example, or as a motif for embroidery. In some schools, children have cut and stitched the flag themselves, or made a cardboard version with cut-outs or collage. The United Nations has published a handbook, *Flags of the United Nations*,[2] containing coloured illustrations of the flags of Member States and giving facts about the origin and meaning of each design. A brief history of the organization, its flag, its aims and ideals is included.

Action projects

It is abundantly clear that the best learning is with the active participation of the students. This involves them more deeply in a subject than reading or listening to an explanation or commentary. It is especially important in education programmes about the United Nations system to provide some kind of action whenever possible.

In a developing nation, this could be helping to build a local

1. *United Nations Postage Stamps*, New York, United Nations, 1956, 88 p.
2. *Flags of the United Nations*, New York, United Nations, 36 p.

school building, 'plant' fish in the village pond, construct a road or bridge, or carry out a campaign for better health in the community. In a wealthier or more industrialized country students can take part in fund-raising activities on behalf of the Unesco Gift Coupon Scheme, the Freedom from Hunger Campaign of the Food and Agriculture Organization, or one of Unicef's projects.

Every effort should be made to ensure that action is not limited to the giving of money, food or clothing. 'Pen-pal' programmes for writing to students in other parts of the world can be developed and school affiliation programmes whereby schools in different countries are linked in long-term friendships with exchange of letters and materials or exchange visits between students and faculty members. These activities come under the wider aspect of education for international understanding but are mentioned here as examples of sharing rather than just giving.

Students can enrich their own school programme by collecting source materials on the United Nations system, helping to prepare an exhibition, planting trees to commemorate the United Nations or as part of the tree planting programme sponsored by the Food and Agriculture Organization.

School assemblies

In many schools the students assemble daily or at least once a week in a convocation or assembly. This allows everyone to attend or take part in lectures, concerts, plays, panel discussions or other activities of interest to the school in general. These occasions could be used for special programmes on the United Nations, including the showing of films and filmstrips, reports from classes studying various parts of the United Nations system, debates and panels, and 'quiz' programmes.

A more ambitious type of programme is the staging of a model assembly of some part of the United Nations as described under the sub-heading 'Model Assemblies' of this chapter.

Suggestions for assembly programmes on the United Nations could well be published by governments, non-governmental organizations, school systems, or teachers' groups. In any country where daily or weekly school assemblies take place, opportunities for learning about the United Nations would be increased for thousands of students.

School and out-of-school clubs

Clubs, societies or study circles are formed in many schools to encourage students to develop their special interests or talents in the company of others with similar tastes. These are usually sponsored by a teacher but run largely by the students who thus acquire valuable experience in conducting meetings and arranging programmes. There are clubs representing all kinds of interests and activities including support for the United Nations and human rights. Some are International Relations Clubs, some Unesco Clubs, and some World Affairs Clubs. They constitute a valuable means for learning about the United Nations family and make a chain round the world of students interested in international relations.

Then there are millions of children and young people who are members of out-of-school clubs of many kinds: Boy Scouts and Girl Guides, Camp Fire Girls, Future Farmers, Future Home-makers, 4H and 4C Groups and semi-political organizations. Some of these groups include work on the United Nations in their activities.

In the 1960 report several references were made to school and out-of-school clubs. Ceylon reported the formation of International Relations Clubs in selected government schools in nine provinces. The United Kingdom described in detail the extensive work done by clubs in British schools, often with the assistance of the Council for Education in World Citizenship. The U.S.S.R., as mentioned earlier, also referred to the work of out-of-school youth groups. The United States reported on many such school groups and on some activities by national out-of-school clubs and youth organizations. Yugoslavia stated that United Nations clubs in primary and middle grades as well as in universities are a focal point for the dissemination of information about the United Nations. Responsibility for these clubs lies with the Union of Yugoslav Students for the United Nations, an affiliate of the International Student Movement for the United Nations.

Excursions and visits

One of the best ways to learn about the United Nations and its related agencies is to visit their headquarters or regional offices. It is possible for school groups from Canada and the United States to visit the United Nations headquarters in New York. In other countries excursions could sometimes be arranged to the headquarters of the specialized agencies. And in many places students could visit the scene of United Nations projects in technical assistance and community development. These visits need to be carefully planned to yield the best results. Some suggestions are highlighted in two publications submitted in governmental reports to the Economic and Social Council. One is *The United Nations in Your High School*,[1] produced by the United Nations Association in Canada, and the other a leaflet, *Your Visit to the United Nations*, prepared by the Committee on International Relations of the National Education Association in the United States.[2]

Conclusion

There are many methods that can be used in studying the United Nations and its related agencies and a fairly wide array of resources, although not nearly as much material as could be desired. Teachers and adult education leaders should be able to plan a wide variety of lessons and activities from the above suggestions and develop extensive, interesting and deep studies of the United Nations family.

1. *The United Nations in Your High School*, Toronto, Canada, United Nations Association, 1960, 14 p.
2. Committee on International Relations, *Your Visit to the United Nations*, Washington, National Education Association, 1959, 13 p.

7 Evaluation of teaching about the United Nations and its related agencies

The most neglected aspect of all teaching about the United Nations system is that of evaluation. It is extremely difficult to ascertain whether desirable results have been obtained in teaching especially if the test of its effectiveness lies perhaps in actions in the distant future or in behaviour that cannot be measured. Evaluation involves many factors in the learning process that cannot be easily isolated and tested. Another difficulty is that few satisfactory instruments have been developed for determining the effectiveness of the teaching-learning process.

Some progress has been made in developing effective methods of evaluation in the much broader topic of education for living in the international community, partly as a result of Unesco's Associated Schools Project. In reports on these schools there are many leads that can be followed profitably.[1]

But very little has been done as yet for teaching about the

1. See, for example, Unesco's booklet on *Education for International Understanding: Examples and Suggestions for Classroom Use*, Paris, Unesco, 1959, Chapter 8 on 'Research and Evaluation'; the Government of India's booklet on *Education for International Understanding and Co-operation*, New Delhi, Ministry of Education, 1959, p. 43-76; or the *Report on the Co-ordinated Experimental Activities in Japan for Education for International Understanding and Co-operation*, Tokyo, Japanese National Commission for Unesco, 1956, p. 193-224.

United Nations family, as is proved by various reports on the subject. The few references made to evaluation are usually passing references to examination questions on the United Nations for secondary school students or for teachers' licences.

Some references, however, are welcome and helpful. In the 1952 report on teaching about the United Nations the Government of the United Kingdom cited a study made in the Walworth Secondary School with students in the 14-15 age-group. In this school students vary widely in aptitude and ability, so the study was not made with a selected group. The staff attempted to use factual tests to determine to what degree knowledge about the United Nations system had been increased, and attitude tests to measure how and in what ways individual attitudes to world problems and the United Nations had been changed by teaching. It was hoped to be able to furnish data to other teachers and to provide United Nations officials with suggestions for suitable materials for teachers and for pupils.

Four conclusions were drawn from this study:

1. Interest in the United Nations can be aroused among 14- and 15-year-old children of varying abilities, if they are properly approached.
2. The best approach seems to be to start with a local problem, extend this to the national level, and then to see the international implications, including the part the United Nations and its agencies play.
3. During the study an attempt should be made to see the inter-relationship of the various parts of the United Nations.
4. It is wrong to begin with the study of the structure of the United Nations. Children of this age have no interest in a detailed examination of the executive and administrative functions of international organizations and such information is meaningless to them at this level.

The 1952 report also referred to a study made in the Liceo Experimental Manuel de Salas in Santiago, Chile, where for a year considerable attention was given in the academic curriculum to the United Nations system with students from 13 to 15 years of age. Among conclusions drawn by the staff were the following:

1. At the beginning of the year students were sceptical about the

work of the United Nations and not particularly interested in it. By the end of the year 100 per cent were interested in varying degrees and supported the United Nations system as the only possible solution to the world's problems.

2. Eighty per cent of the students understood by the end of the year why the United Nations could not solve all the major political problems. Twenty per cent were still unable to see why it could not accomplish more.

3. Literature on the United Nations stressing the human element, such as biographical and anecdotal stories of personal participation in its activities, aroused interest more effectively than material on theories and structure.

4. There was increased knowledge of and interest in geography. In the 1956 report there is special reference to an evaluation of materials prepared for teaching about the United Nations but the 1960 report is almost devoid of comments on the subject. Undoubtedly there have been a number of experiments in evaluating learning about the United Nations and its agencies, but they have not been included in reports to the Economic and Social Council. It is to be hoped that in future all such experiments will be reported so that educators everywhere can profit.

The word evaluation is used here because it is a more inclusive term than measurement. It is relatively easy to measure the acquisition of knowledge and its retention over at least a short period of time. It is much more difficult to determine accurately interest in the United Nations family or parts of it, skills in reading about, analysing and interpreting it, and attitudes towards it. But these are an integral part of a proper evaluation of learning.

It is also certain that, for any effective evaluation, teaching must be very clear in its aims. It is impossible to evaluate results if the aims to be tested are not as definite and distinct as possible. This is an involved and complicated subject which needs much study. Some could be carried out by teachers, school systems and governments, but more should be done by people with expert knowledge of evaluation procedures and instruments. In the meantime, educators will have to proceed with the limited knowledge we have on ways of evaluating teaching about the United Nations family. Let us look at some of these.

It is relatively easy to test factual information about the United Nations. This can be done quickly and efficiently, for example, by the use of multiple-choice questions such as this:

The United Nations was formed at a conference held in 1945 in Moscow . . . London . . . Geneva . . . San Francisco . . . Or it can be done with questions to be completed such as the following:

The title given to the head of the United Nations Secretariat is . . . . Since such facts can be quickly forgotten it would be interesting and valuable to give the same test six months later to see which have been retained. Teachers could then attempt to determine why some facts were remembered and others forgotten. Short essays may also be used to test knowledge.

A much more difficult method of evaluation, intended to test a student's ability to think in terms of the United Nations system, is the writing of 'position papers' on a problem with which the United Nations or one of its agencies or commissions deals. These can be prepared as research papers or in response to a test question. They require much more depth of understanding and data than most types of essay questions. An example would be for a student to draft a report as if he were a member of the United Nations Secretariat. It might be on the lack of water in some region and the efforts of the United Nations to help the community with the problem, or on the various plans for disarmament and the pros and cons of the attitudes of different countries.

Another test is the writing of a speech the President of the General Assembly might give at the opening session of an Assembly. This would require a deep understanding of the crucial issues before the United Nations and a knowledge of the background of the President of that session.

Such papers could be saved and returned to students a few weeks or months later to be rewritten in the light of further information and deeper understanding of the United Nations system.

A simplified version of this approach is for the teacher to present a document containing some incorrect information and distorted statements. The students are asked to criticize and rewrite the document.

Specialists in evaluation frequently stress the value of open-ended questions or statements. One use of this method is to ask students at the beginning of a study to complete the simple statement, 'The United Nations is . . . . . .'. At the end of their study they are asked to do the same exercise. There are two merits in this method. One is to give teachers an understanding of what students do or do not know at the beginning of a series of lessons and the other to give them a comparison of what students write at the beginning and end of a study of the United Nations family. A variation of this is for children to draw pictures of their idea of the United Nations. This, too, can be done before and after an organized study.

It is also important to evaluate resources as well as knowledge and attitudes. A good many groups have commented over the years on the effectiveness of materials on the United Nations and its agencies which they have used. But the most ambitious undertaking of this kind was a report made in the United Kingdom in 1956 by an *ad hoc* committee of the National Commission for Unesco. It covered publications, films and filmstrips issued by the United Nations, Unesco and the other specialized agencies.[1] It is a lengthy report that cannot be described in detail here, but among its many conclusions and recommendations are the following:

1. Examples of the United Nations at work in specific situations are highly desirable. Such examples are to be found in a few publications but these are not widely distributed or well known.
2. Achievements need to be measured in terms of what remains to be done as well as what has already happened.
3. The vocabulary of publications, films and filmstrips needs to be simplified and technical jargon omitted as much as possible.
4. The special issues of *The Unesco Courier* on such topics as 'Refugees', 'Killers of the Insect World', and 'Latin America' are prime examples of the type of materials schools need.

---

1. T. Ivor Davies, *Report on Materials and Aids available from United Nations Sources for Teaching about the Activities of the United Nations and the Specialized Agencies in Secondary Schools in the United Kingdom*, New York, United Nations, 1956, 36 p. Mimeographed document UN 7(9)/4.

5. Photographs and posters need to stress people much more than they have done.
6. Films and filmstrips need to concentrate on a single area, topic or problem. Films should be short (preferably fifteen or twenty minutes) to permit time for class discussions.

These highlights from the report should be helpful to governments, organizations and individuals preparing material on the United Nations and its related agencies. They are by no means the only pertinent suggestions made in this provocative and useful document.

If teachers and other educators are really interested in the effectiveness of teaching materials they should attempt to get the frank reactions of readers and viewers. Sometimes this can be done by discussions on the value of such materials. Often it can be done by brief, written comments by the people who have read a book or seen a film or filmstrip. A more honest response will generally be elicited by an anonymous check-list including items like the following:

1. I found this book:
   Very interesting ...... Interesting ...... Fair ...... Dull ......
2. The pictures in it were:
   Very interesting ...... Interesting ...... Fair ...... Dull ......
3. The words the author used were:
   All right ...... Too difficult ...... Too easy ......
4. I would recommend this book (check one or two items):
   To students my age ......
   To students older than I am ......
   To students younger than I am ......
   To people who are really interested in this subject ......

Another method of evaluating progress or lack of it is to talk to people other than the students involved. Parents, other teachers and librarians are among those who will often discover more about the reactions of students to a topic being studied than the teacher in charge.

Because so little has been done in the broad field of evaluating teaching about the United Nations system there are many opportunities for graduate students, especially in teacher-training institutions, to work on the subject. Their studies should be disseminated widely through professional journals and in reports of Member States to the United Nations and Unesco.

The evaluation of teaching about the United Nations and its related agencies is crucial. It calls for a vast amount of study and experimentation by competent persons in all countries.

8   Conclusions and suggestions

All the evidence available indicates that great strides have been made in recent years in extending teaching about the United Nations and its related agencies and in deepening existing studies. A wide variety of methods has been used to improve such instruction and a large number of resources have been developed by individuals, teachers' groups, non-governmental organizations and governments, as well as by various agencies in the United Nations family, to enrich teaching about the United Nations system.

But there is a great deal to do before educators can claim that they are reaching even a majority of the children and young people in schools and institutions of higher learning, the millions of them who do not attend schools and the vast numbers of adults everywhere. Pride in past and present achievements should not blind anyone to the fact that the surface of this new task in education has scarcely been scratched.

Interested people, organizations and institutions in all countries should consider what needs to be done to further teaching about the United Nations and its agencies. They should:
1. Examine even more closely than in the past the aims and purposes of education about the United Nations and its related agencies in an effort to clarify the aims of such teaching.
2. Attempt to determine to what extent knowledge about the United Nations family is the aim of such teaching and to what

extent attitudes towards these organizations should be considered as one of its aims.

3. Continue to encourage teaching about the United Nations and its agencies through the use of directives from national Ministries of Education and other appropriate bodies in countries where this is the common practice for changing the curricula.

4. Implement such directives as far as possible in as many ways as possible.

5. Extend and deepen the studies of the United Nations family made by prospective teachers of all grade levels and all subjects.

6. Study the possibilities of further in-service education of teachers, especially by the use of seminars or workshops locally, nationally and regionally, and in co-operation with non-governmental organizations interested in the United Nations system.

7. Determine what aspects of the United Nations and its related agencies can be taught most appropriately at different age levels in schools.

8. Examine the need for teaching about the United Nations system in the early years of school, in the light of changing world conditions, and in view of the fact that many children drop out of school within a few years of their initial enrolment.

9. Examine the possibilities of including some aspects of the work of the United Nations and its agencies in many school subjects.

10. Increase the amount of teaching about the United Nations system in institutions of higher learning and encourage mature students to study in depth some of the major problems with which the United Nations and its agencies are wrestling.

11. Explore ways and means of reaching the vast adult population with educational programmes regarding the United Nations system, using particularly the mass media of communication, such as films, radio and television.

12. Encourage non-school agencies to co-operate in teaching about the United Nations family, especially in communities where only a small percentage of the children and youth are in school.

13. Suggest to educators the variety of methods that can be used effectively in the presentation of the many aspects of the United Nations system and encourage them to experiment with ways of presenting this part of their teaching.

14. Encourage sustained and continued teaching about the United Nations family throughout the school year, rather than the prevailing practice of giving attention to the United Nations solely or chiefly on United Nations Day or during United Nations Week.

15. Provide examples of effective teaching about the United Nations and its agencies: printed descriptions of promising practices, demonstration lessons and diagrammatic accounts.

16. Encourage inclusion of essay-type questions on the United Nations in important external examinations, such as school-leaving, matriculation, and college and university entrance examinations.

17. Invite the various specialized agencies to explore ways of teaching about their part of the United Nations system, working in co-operation with teachers and with appropriate personnel of the United Nations and Unesco.

18. Encourage the publication of brief readable accounts of the United Nations for various age levels, stressing the human element and concentrating on the work of the United Nations system in countries and regions of the world as well as on problems.

19. Arrange for the inclusion of effective sections on the United Nations family in relevant school textbooks, particularly in the fields of geography, history, civics and social studies, especially when revised or new editions are being produced.

20. Encourage well-known writers for children, youth and adults to avail themselves of the facilities of the United Nations system in the preparation of reading materials on the United Nations and its related agencies.

21. Promote the publication of brief accounts by United Nations interpreters and translators of their work for use primarily, but not solely, in language classes.

22. Prepare more materials of a biographical nature on men and women who have contributed or are contributing to the work

of the United Nations system and of the people who have been or are being assisted by the United Nations and its agencies.

23. Further the production and use of audio-visual materials for teaching about the United Nations in school and out-of-school agencies with special reference to pictures, posters, radio and television.

24. Investigate the possibilities of kits of materials for teachers and other educators, particularly for young teachers leaving teacher training institutions for their first jobs.

25. Explore ways and means of evaluating teaching about the United Nations family, especially in pilot schools working intensively in this field, and publish the findings.

26. Continue to elicit the support of administrative officials and the general public in support of school and out-of-school education about the United Nations and its related agencies.

A good many suggestions have been offered above in the hope that different individuals, groups and governments will act on those which seem most important and relevant to them. It is hoped they will report their efforts to the appropriate bodies so that others may profit from their experiences.

To reach every citizen of the Member States of the United Nations and its related agencies and to inform them about the work of this vitally important and complex international organization so that they may become intelligent supporters of its work, is a vast responsibility for educators everywhere. But it is also a thrilling and exciting challenge and imperative for effective living in this second half of the twentieth century.

Appendixes

1

Excerpt from the Charter of the United Nations

We the peoples of the United Nations determined

To save succeeding generations from the scourge of war, which twice in our lifetime has brought untold sorrow to mankind, and

To reaffirm faith in fundamental human rights, in the dignity and worth of the human person, in the equal rights of men and women and of nations large and small, and

To establish conditions under which justice and respect for the obligations arising from treaties and other sources of international law can be maintained, and

To promote social progress and better standards of life in larger freedom,

And for these ends

To practice tolerance and live together in peace with one another as good neighbors, and

To unite our strength to maintain international peace and security, and

To ensure, by the acceptance of principles and the institution of methods, that armed force shall not be used, save in the common interest, and

To employ international machinery for the promotion of the economic and social advancement of all peoples,

*Have resolved to combine our efforts
to accomplish these aims*

Accordingly, our respective Governments, through representatives assembled in the city of San Francisco, who have exhibited their full powers found to be in good and due form, have agreed to the present Charter of the United Nations and do hereby establish an international organization to be known as the United Nations.

Article 1   *Purposes and principles*

The Purposes of the United Nations are:

1. To maintain international peace and security, and to that end: to take effective collective measures for the prevention and removal of threats to the peace, and for the suppression of acts of aggression or other breaches of the peace, and to bring about by peaceful means, and in conformity with the principles of justice and international law, adjustment or settlement of international disputes or situations which might lead to a breach of the peace;

2. To develop friendly relations among nations based on respect for the principle of equal rights and self-determination of peoples, and to take other appropriate measures to strengthen universal peace;

3. To achieve international co-operation in solving international problems of an economic, social, cultural, or humanitarian character, and in promoting and encouraging respect for human rights and for fundamental freedoms for all without distinction as to race, sex, language, or religion; and

4. To be a center for harmonizing the actions of nations in the attainment of these common ends.

2

Excerpt from the Constitution of the United Nations Educational, Scientific and Cultural Organization

The Governments of the States Parties to this Constitution on behalf of their peoples declare:

That since wars begin in the minds of men, it is in the minds of men that the defences of peace must be constructed;

That ignorance of each other's ways and lives has been a common cause, throughout the history of mankind, of that suspicion and mistrust between the peoples of the world through which their differences have all too often broken into war;

That the great and terrible war which has now ended was a war made possible by the denial of the democratic principles of the dignity, equality and mutual respect of men, and by the propagation, in their place, through ignorance and prejudice, of the doctrine of the inequality of men and races;

That the wide diffusion of culture, and the education of humanity for justice and liberty and peace are indispensable to the dignity of man and constitute a sacred duty which all the nations must fulfil in a spirit of mutual assistance and concern;

That a peace based exclusively upon the political and economic arrangements of governments would not be a peace which could secure the unanimous, lasting and sincere support of the peoples of the world, and that the peace must therefore be founded, if it is not to fail, upon the intellectual and moral solidarity of mankind.

For these reasons, the States Parties to this Constitution, believing in full and equal opportunities for education for all, in the unrestricted pursuit of objective truth, and in the free exchange of ideas and knowledge, are agreed and determined to develop and to increase the means of communication between their peoples and to employ these means for the purposes of mutual understanding and a truer and more perfect knowledge of each other's lives;

In consequence whereof they do hereby create the United Nations Educational, Scientific and Cultural Organization for the purpose of advancing, through the educational and scientific and cultural relations of the peoples of the world, the objectives of international peace and of the common welfare of mankind for which the United Nations Organization was established and which its Charter proclaims.

Article 1   *Purposes and functions*

1. The purpose of the Organization is to contribute to peace and security by promoting collaboration among the nations through education, science and culture in order to further universal respect for justice, for the rule of law and for the human rights and fundamental freedoms which are affirmed for the peoples of the world, without distinction of race, sex, language or religion by the Charter of the United Nations.

2. To realize this purpose the Organization will:

a. Collaborate in the work of advancing the mutual knowledge and understanding of peoples, through all means of mass communication and to that end recommend such international agreements as may be necessary to promote the free flow of ideas by word and image;

b. Give fresh impulse to popular education and to the spread of culture; by collaborating with Members, at their request, in the development of educational activities;

by instituting collaboration among the nations to advance the ideal of equality of educational opportunity without regard to race, sex or any distinctions, economic or social;

by suggesting educational methods best suited to prepare the children of the world for the responsibilities of freedom;

c. Maintain, increase and diffuse knowledge;

by assuring the conservation and protection of the world's inheritance of books, works of art and monuments of history and science, and recommending to the nations concerned the necessary international conventions;

by encouraging co-operation among the nations in all branches of intellectual activity, including the international exchange of persons active in the fields of education, science and culture and the exchange of publications, objects of artistic and scientific interest and other materials of information; by initiating methods of international co-operation calculated to give the people of all countries access to the printed and published materials produced by any of them.

3. With a view to preserving the independence, integrity and fruitful diversity of the cultures and educational systems of the States members of this Organization, the Organization is prohibited from intervening in matters which are essentially within their domestic jurisdiction.

3

Universal Declaration of Human Rights

Preamble

Whereas recognition of the inherent dignity and of the equal and inalienable rights of all members of the human family is the foundation of freedom, justice and peace in the world,

Whereas disregard and contempt for human rights have resulted in barbarous acts which have outraged the conscience of mankind, and the advent of a world in which human beings shall enjoy freedom of speech and belief and freedom from fear and want has been proclaimed as the highest aspiration of the common people,

Whereas it is essential, if man is not to be compelled to have recourse, as a last resort, to rebellion against tyranny and oppression, that human rights should be protected by the rule of law,

Whereas it is essential to promote the development of friendly relations between nations,

Whereas the peoples of the United Nations have in the Charter reaffirmed their faith in fundamental human rights, in the dignity and worth of the human person and in the equal rights of men and women and have determined to promote social progress and better standards of life in larger freedom,

Whereas Member States have pledged themselves to achieve, in co-operation with the United Nations, the promotion of universal respect for and observance of human rights and fundamental freedoms,

Whereas a common understanding of these rights and freedoms is of the greatest importance for the full realization of this pledge,

Now, therefore,
The General Assembly
proclaims

This Universal Declaration of Human Rights as a common standard of achievement for all peoples and all nations, to the end that every individual and every organ of society, keeping this Declaration constantly in mind, shall strive by teaching and education to promote respect for these rights and freedoms and by progressive measures, national and international, to secure their universal and effective recognition and observance, both among the peoples of Member States themselves and among the peoples of territories under their jurisdiction.

Article 1. All human beings are born free and equal in dignity and rights. They are endowed with reason and conscience and should act towards one another in a spirit of brotherhood.

Article 2. Everyone is entitled to all the rights and freedoms set forth in this Declaration, without distinction of any kind, such as race, colour, sex, language, religion, political or other opinion, national or social origin, property, birth or other status.

Furthermore, no distinction shall be made on the basis of the political, jurisdictional or international status of the country or territory to which a person belongs, whether it be independent, trust, non-self-governing or under any other limitation of sovereignty.

Article 3. Everyone has the right to life, liberty and security of person.

Article 4. No one shall be held in slavery or servitude; slavery and the slave trade shall be prohibited in all their forms.

Article 5. No one shall be subjected to torture or to cruel, inhuman or degrading treatment or punishment.

Article 6. Everyone has the right to recognition everywhere as a person before the law.

Article 7. All are equal before the law and are entitled without any discrimination to equal protection of the law. All are entitled to equal protection against any discrimination in violation of this Declaration and against any incitement to such discrimination.

Article 8. Everyone has the right to an effective remedy by the competent national tribunals for acts violating the fundamental rights granted him by the constitution or by law.

Article 9. No one shall be subjected to arbitrary arrest, detention or exile.

Article 10. Everyone is entitled in full equality to a fair and public hearing by an independent and impartial tribunal, in the determination of his rights and obligations and of any criminal charge against him.

Article 11. (1) Everyone charged with a penal offence has the right to be presumed innocent until proved guilty according to law in a public trial at which he has had all the guarantees necessary for his defence.

(2) No one shall be held guilty of any penal offence on account of any act or omission which did not constitute a penal offence, under national or international law, at the time when it was committed. Nor shall a heavier penalty be imposed than the one that was applicable at the time the penal offence was committed.

Article 12. No one shall be subjected to arbitrary interference with his privacy, family, home or correspondence, nor to attacks upon his honour and reputation. Everyone has the right to the protection of the law against such interference or attacks.

Article 13. (1) Everyone has the right to freedom of movement and residence within the borders of each state.

(2) Everyone has the right to leave any country, including his own, and to return to his country.

Article 14. (1) Everyone has the right to seek and to enjoy in other countries asylum from persecution.

(2) This right may not be invoked in the case of prosecutions genuinely arising from non-political crimes or from acts contrary to the purposes and principles of the United Nations.

Article 15. (1) Everyone has the right to a nationality.

(2) No one shall be arbitrarily deprived of his nationality nor denied the right to change his nationality.

Article 16. (1) Men and women of full age, without any limitation due to race, nationality or religion, have the right to marry and to found a family. They are entitled to equal rights as to marriage, during marriage and at its dissolution.

(2) Marriage shall be entered into only with the free and full consent of the intending spouses.

(3) The family is the natural and fundamental group unit of society and is entitled to protection by society and the State.

Article 17. (1) Everyone has the right to own property alone as well as in association with others.

(2) No one shall be arbitrarily deprived of his property.

Article 18. Everyone has the right to freedom of thought, conscience and religion ; this right includes freedom to change his religion or belief, and freedom, either alone or in community with others and in public or private, to manifest his religion of belief in teaching, practice, worship and observance.

Article 19. Everyone has the right to freedom of opinion and expression ; this right includes freedom to hold opinions without interference and to seek, receive and impart information and ideas through any media and regardless of frontiers.

Article 20. (1) Everyone has the right to freedom of peaceful assembly and association.

(2) No one may be compelled to belong to an association.

Article 21. (1) Everyone has the right to take part in the government of his country, directly or through freely chosen representatives.

(2) Everyone has the right of equal access to public service in his country.

(3) The will of the people shall be the basis of the authority of government ; this will shall be expressed in periodic and genuine elections which shall be by universal and equal suffrage and shall be held by secret vote or by equivalent free voting procedures.

Article 22. Everyone, as a member of society, has the right to social security and is entitled to realization, through national effort and international co-operation and in accordance with the organization and resources of each State, of the economic, social and cultural rights indispensable for his dignity and the free development of his personality.

Article 23. (1) Everyone has the right to work, to free choice of employment, to just and favourable conditions of work and to protection against unemployment.

(2) Everyone, without any discrimination, has the right to equal pay for equal work.

(3) Everyone who works has the right to just and favourable remuneration ensuring for himself and his family an existence worthy of human dignity, and supplemented, if necessary, by other means of social protection.

(4) Everyone has the right to form and to join trade unions for the protection of his interests.

Article 24. Everyone has the right to rest and leisure, including reasonable limitation of working hours and periodic holidays with pay.

Article 25. (1) Everyone has the right to a standard of living adequate for the health and well-being of himself and of his family, including food, clothing, housing and medical care and necessary social services, and the right to security in the event of unemployment, sickness, disability, widowhood, old age or other lack of livelihood in circumstances beyond his control.

(2) Motherhood and childhood are entitled to special care and assistance. All children, whether born in or out of wedlock, shall enjoy the same social protection.

Article 26. (1) Everyone has the right to education. Education shall be free, at least in the elementary and fundamental stages. Elementary education shall be compulsory. Technical and professional education shall be made generally available and higher education shall be equally accessible to all on the basis of merit.

(2) Education shall be directed to the full development of the human personality and to the strengthening of respect for human rights and fundamental freedoms. It shall promote understanding, tolerance and friendship among all nations, racial or religious groups, and shall further the activities of the United Nations for the maintenance of peace.

(3) Parents have a prior right to choose the kind of education that shall be given to their children.

Article 27. (1) Everyone has the right freely to participate in the cultural life of the community, to enjoy the arts and to share in scientific advancement and its benefits.

(2) Everyone has the right to the protection of the moral and material interests resulting from any scientific, literary or artistic production of which he is the author.

Article 28. Everyone is entitled to a social and international order in which the rights and freedoms set forth in this Declaration can be fully realized.

Article 29. (1) Everyone has duties to the community in which alone the free and full development of his personality is possible.

(2) In the exercise of his rights and freedoms, everyone shall be subject only to such limitations as are determined by law solely for the purpose of securing due recognition and respect for the rights and freedoms of others and of meeting the just requirements of morality, public order and the general welfare in a democratic society.

(3) These rights and freedoms may in no case be exercised contrary to the purposes and principles of the United Nations.

Article 30. Nothing in this Declaration may be interpreted as implying for any State, group or person any right to engage in any activity or to perform any act aimed at the destruction of any of the rights and freedoms set forth herein.

4

Declaration of the Rights of the Child

Preamble

Whereas the peoples of the United Nations have, in the Charter, reaffirmed their faith in fundamental human rights, and in the dignity and worth of the human person, and have determined to promote social progress and better standards of life in larger freedom,

Whereas the United Nations has, in the Universal Declaration of Human Rights, proclaimed that everyone is entitled to all the rights and freedoms set forth therein, without distinction of any kind, such as race, color, sex, language, religion, political or other opinion, national or social origin, property, birth or other status,

Whereas the child, by reason of his physical and mental immaturity, needs special safeguards and care, including appropriate legal protection, before as well as after birth,

Whereas the need for such special safeguards has been stated in the Geneva Declaration of the Rights of the Child of 1924, and recognized in the Universal Declaration of Human Rights and in the statutes of specialized agencies and international organizations concerned with the welfare of children,

Whereas mankind owes to the child the best it has to give,

Now, therefore,
The General Assembly
proclaims

This Declaration of the Rights of the Child to the end that he may
have a happy childhood and enjoy for his own good and for the good
of society the rights and freedoms herein set forth, and calls upon
parents, upon men and women as individuals and upon voluntary
organizations, local authorities and national governments to recognize
these rights and strive for their observance by legislature and other
measures progressively taken in accordance with the following principles :

Principle 1

The child shall enjoy all the rights set forth in this Declaration. All
children, without any exception whatsoever, shall be entitled to these
rights, without distinction or discrimination on account of race, color,
sex, language, religion, political or other opinion, national or social
origin, property, birth or other status, whether of himself or of his
family.

Principle 2

The child shall enjoy special protection, and shall be given opportunities
and facilities, by law and by other means, to enable him to develop
physically, mentally, morally, spiritually and socially in a healthy and
normal manner and in conditions of freedom and dignity. In the
enactment of laws for this purpose the best interests of the child shall
be the paramount consideration.

Principle 3

The child shall be entitled from his birth to a name and a nationality.

Principle 4

The child shall enjoy the benefits of social security. He shall be entitled
to grow and develop in health ; to this end special care and protection
shall be provided both to him and to his mother, including adequate
pre-natal and post-natal care. The child shall have the right to adequate
nutrition, housing, recreation and medical services.

Principle 5

The child who is physically, mentally or socially handicapped shall be
given the special treatment, education and care required by his particular condition.

Principle 6

The child, for the full and harmonious development of his personality, needs love and understanding. He shall, wherever possible, grow up in the care and under the responsibility of his parents, and in any case in an atmosphere of affection and of moral and material security; a child of tender years shall not, save in exceptional circumstances, be separated from his mother. Society and the public authorities shall have the duty to extend particular care to children without a family and to those without adequate means of support. Payment of state and other assistance toward the maintenance of children of large families is desirable.

Principle 7

The child is entitled to receive education, which shall be free and compulsory, at least in the elementary stages. He shall be given an education which will promote his general culture, and enable him on a basis of equal opportunity to develop his abilities, his individual judgement, and his sense of moral and social responsibility, and to become a useful member of society.

The best interests of the child shall be the guiding principle of those responsible for his education and guidance; that responsibility lies in the first place with his parents.

The child shall have full opportunity for play and recreation, which should be directed to the same purposes as education; society and the public authorities shall endeavor to promote the enjoyment of this right.

Principle 8

The child shall in all circumstances be among the first to receive protection and relief.

Principle 9

The child shall be protected against all forms of neglect, cruelty and exploitation. He shall not be the subject of traffic, in any form.

The child shall not be admitted to employment before an appropriate minimum age; he shall in no case be caused or permitted to engage in any occupation or employment which would prejudice his health or education, or interfere with his physical, mental or moral development.

Principle 10

The child shall be protected from practices which may foster racial, religious and any other form of discrimination. He shall be brought up in a spirit of understanding, tolerance, friendship among peoples, peace and universal brotherhood and in full consciousness that his energy and talents should be devoted to the service of his fellow men.

5

Addresses of Organizations

United Nations Information Centres / Offices

Accra. United Nations Information Centre, Post Box 2339, Accra, Ghana.
Street address: Liberia and Maxwell Roads.
Area covered: Gambia, Ghana, Guinea, Nigeria, Sierra Leone.

Addis Ababa. ECA Information Officer: United Nations Information Office, United Nations Economic Commission for Africa, P.O. Box 3001, Addis Ababa, Ethiopia.
Street address: Adua Square.
Area covered: Ethiopia.

Asunción. Centro de Información de las Naciones Unidas, Calle Chile 430, Apartado postal 1107, Asunción, Paraguay.
Area covered: Paraguay.

Athens. United Nations Information Centre, 25A Jan Smuts Street, Athens, Greece.
Area covered: Cyprus, Greece, Israel, Turkey.

Baghdad. United Nations Information Centre, P.O. Box 2048, Baghdad, Iraq.
Area covered: Iraq.

Bangkok. Information Service: Chief of Information Service, Economic Commission for Asia and the Far East, Sala Santitham, Bangkok, Thailand.
Area covered: Cambodia, Laos, Federation of Malaya and Singapore, Thailand, Viet-Nam.

Beirut. United Nations Information Centre, P.O. Box 4656, Beirut, Lebanon.
Area covered: Jordan, Lebanon, Syria.

Belgrade. United Nations Information Centre, P.O. Box 157, Belgrade, Yugoslavia.
Street address: Trg. Marksa i Engelsa, br. 1.
Area covered: Albania, Yugoslavia.

Bogotá. Centro de Información de las Naciones Unidas, P.O. Box 65-67, Bogotá, Colombia.
Street address: Calle 19, Numero 7-30-Septimo Piso.
Area covered: Colombia, Ecuador, Venezuela.

Buenos Aires. Centro de Información de las Naciones Unidas, Marcelo T. de Alvear 684, 3F, Buenos Aires, Argentina.
Area covered: Argentina, Uruguay.

Cairo. United Nations Information Centre, Sharia El Shams, Imm, Tagher, B.P. 262, Garden City, Cairo, United Arab Republic.
Area covered: Saudi Arabia, Sudan, United Arab Republic, Yemen.

Colombo. United Nations Information Centre, 45 Alfred House Gardens, Colombo 3 (P.O. Box 1505), Ceylon.
Area covered: Ceylon.

Copenhagen. United Nations Information Centre, 37 H. C. Andersens Boulevard, Copenhagen V, Denmark.
Area covered: Denmark, Finland, Iceland, Norway, Sweden.

Dar-es-Salaam. United Nations Information Centre, P.O. Box 9182, Dar-es-Salaam, Tanganyika.
Area covered: Kenya, Northern Rhodesia, Nyasaland, Tanganyika, Uganda, Zanzibar.

Geneva. (Information Service of the Geneva Office, United Nations): Information Service, European Office, Palais des Nations, Geneva, Switzerland.
Area covered: Austria, Bulgaria, Germany, Hungary, Poland, Rumania, Switzerland.

Jakarta. United Nations Information Centre, 76 Kebon Sirih, Jakarta, Indonesia.
Area covered: Indonesia.

Kabul. United Nations Information Office, P.O. Box 5, Kabul, Afghanistan.
Street address: Shah Mahmoud, Ghazi Square.
Area covered: Afghanistan.

Karachi. United Nations Information Centre, P.O. Box No. 349, G.P.O., Karachi 1, Pakistan.
Street address: Havelock Road.
Area covered: Pakistan.

Lima. United Nations Information Centre, Parque Mariscal Caceres No. 18, Apartado 4480, Lima, Peru.
Area covered: Bolivia, Peru.

Lomé. United Nations Information Centre, Lomé, Togo.

London. United Nations Information Centre, 14/15 Stratford Place, London, W.1, United Kingdom.
Area covered: Ireland, Netherlands, United Kingdom and dependencies except those listed under the Accra, Bangkok, Dar-es-Salaam and Port of Spain centres.

Manila. United Nations Information Centre, P.O. Box 2149, Manila, Philippines.
Street address: World Health Organization, Regional Office of the Western Pacific, corner of Taft Avenue and Isaac Pavel.
Area covered: The Philippines.

Mexico City. Centro de Información de las Naciones Unidas, Hamburgo 63, 3er piso, México 6, D.F., Mexico.
Area covered: Cuba, Dominican Republic, Mexico.

Monrovia. United Nations Information Office, P.O. Box 274, Monrovia, Liberia.
Street address: 24 Broad Street.
Area covered: Liberia.

Moscow. United Nations Information Centre, 15 Hohlovski Pereulok, Apartment 36, Moscow, U.S.S.R.
Area covered: Byelorussian S.S.R., Ukrainian S.S.R., U.S.S.R.

New Delhi. United Nations Information Centre, 21 Curzon Road, New Delhi, India.
Area covered: India, Nepal.

Paris. Centre d'Information des Nations Unies, 26, avenue de Segur, Paris-7e, France.
Area covered: Belgium, France, Luxembourg.

Port Moresby. United Nations Information Centre, c/o Island Products Ltd. Building, Champion Parade, Port Moresby, Papua, New Guinea.
Area covered: New Guinea, Papua.

Port of Spain. United Nations Information Centre, 19 Keate Street, Port of Spain, Trinidad, W. I.
Area covered: British Guiana, British Honduras, Caribbean area.

Prague. United Nations Information Centre, Panska 5, Prague II, Czechoslovakia.
Area covered: Czechoslovakia.

Rabat. United Nations Information Centre, c/o Resident Representative, Technical Assistance Board, Boîte Postale 524, Chellah, Rabat, Morocco.
Area covered: Morocco.

Rangoon. United Nations Information Centre, 24 B Manawhari Road, Rangoon, Burma.
Area covered: Burma.

Rio de Janeiro. United Nations Information Centre, Caixa Postal 1750, Rio de Janeiro, Brazil.
Street address: Rua México 11, Sala 1502.
Area covered: Brazil.

Rome. United Nations Information Centre, Palazzetto Venezia, Piazza San Marco 51, Rome, Italy.
Area covered: Italy.

San Salvador. Centro de Información de las Naciones Unidas, Apartado Postal 1114, San Salvador, El Salvador.
Street address: Edificio de la Gran Logia Cuscatlan, 8a Avenida Sur, Número 126.
Area covered: Costa Rica, El Salvador, Guatemala, Honduras, Nicaragua, Panama.

Santiago. ECLA Information Officer: Economic Commission for Latin America, Avenida Providencia 871, Santiago, Chile.
Area covered: Chile.

Sydney. United Nations Information Centre, Box 4030, General Post Office, Sydney, Australia.
Street address: 44 Martin Place.
Area covered: Australia, New Zealand.

Tananarive. United Nations Information Centre, Boîte Postale 1348, Tananarive, Madagascar.
Area covered: Madagascar.

Teheran. United Nations Information Centre, P.O. Box 1555, Kh. Takhte-Jamshid, 12 Kh. Bendar Pahlavi, Teheran, Iran.
Area covered: Iran.

Tokyo. United Nations Information Centre, New Ohtemachi Building, Room 210, 4, 2-chome, Ohtemachi, Chiyoda-ku, Tokyo, Japan.
Area covered: Japan.

Tunis. United Nations Information Centre, Boîte Postale 863, Tunis, Tunisia.
Street address: 61 Fared Hached, Tunis.

Usumbura. United Nations Information Centre, Boîte Postale 1490, Usumbura, Burundi.
Area covered: Ruanda, Burundi.

Washington. United Nations Information Centre, Suite 714, 1028 Connecticut Avenue, N.W., Washington 6, D.C.

Information Offices of the United Nations and Related Agencies

United Nations. Office of Public Information, United Nations, New York, N.Y., U.S.A.

United Nations Children's Fund. Public Information Officer, Unicef, Room 2410 B, United Nations, New York, N.Y., U.S.A.

International Atomic Energy Agency. Kaerntnerring 11, Vienna I, Austria.

High Commissioner's Office for Refugees. Palais des Nations, Geneva, Switzerland.

International Labour Organisation. Public Information Division, International Labour Organisation, 154, rue de Lausanne, Geneva, Switzerland.
ILO Branch Office, avenida Presidente R. Saenz Pena 615 (piso 7º). Buenos Aires, Argentina.
ILO Branch Office, Reparticão International de Trabalho, Edificio do Ministerio de Trabalho, 2º andar, salas 216 a 220, avenida Presidente Antonio Carlos 251, Rio de Janeiro, Brazil.
ILO Branch Office, Room 307, 202 Queen Street, Ottawa 4, Ontario, Canada.
ILO Branch Office, 205, boulevard Saint-Germain, Paris-7e, France.
ILO Branch Office, Hohenzollernstrasse 21 Bad Godesberg, Bonn, Germany (Federal Republic).
ILO Branch Office, 1-Mandi House, New Delhi, India.
ILO Branch Office, Villa Aldobrandini, 28 Via Panisperna, Rome, Italy.

ILO Branch Office, Zenkoku-Choson-Kaikan, 17 1-chome, Nagatacho, Chiyoda-ku, Tokyo, Japan.

ILO Branch Office, Petrovka 15, Apt. 23, Moscow K 9, U.S.S.R.

ILO Branch Office, 1 Talaat Harb Street, Soussa Building, Flat 83, Cairo, United Arab Republic.

ILO Branch Office, 38-39 Parliament Street, London, S.W.1, United Kingdom.

ILO Branch Office, 917 15th Street, N.W., Washington 5, D.C., U.S.A.

Food and Agriculture Organization. Food and Agriculture Organization of the United Nations, Viale delle Terme de Caracalla, Rome, Italy.

FAO Regional Office for Europe, Palais des Nations, Geneva, Switzerland.

FAO Near East Regional Office, P.O. Box 2223, Cairo, United Arab Republic.

FAO Regional Office for Asia and the Far East, Maliwan Mansion, Phra Atit Road, Bangkok, Thailand.

FAO Regional Office for Asia and the Far East, Western Zone, 21 Curzon Road, New Delhi, India.

FAO Regional Office for Latin America, Northern Zone, Apartado Postal 10778, México (1) D.F., Mexico.

FAO Regional Office for Latin America, Eastern Zone, Rua Jardim Botanico 1008, Rio de Janeiro, Brazil.

FAO Regional Office for Latin America, Western Zone, Casilla 10095, Santiago, Chile.

FAO North American Regional Office, 1325 C Street, S.W., Washington 25, D.C., U.S.A.

FAO Regional Office for Africa, P.O. Box 1628, Accra, Ghana.

United Nations Educational, Scientific and Cultural Organization. Department of Mass Communication, Unesco, Place de Fontenoy, Paris-7e, France.

World Health Organization. Division of Public Information, WHO, Palais des Nations, Geneva, Switzerland.

Regional Office of WHO for Europe, 8 Scherfigsvej, Copenhagen, Denmark.

Public Information Officer, WHO Regional Office for the Americas, Pan-American Sanitary Bureau, 1501 New Hampshire Avenue, N.W., Washington 6, D.C., U.S.A.

Public Information Officer, Regional Office of WHO Eastern Mediterranean, P.O. Box 1517, Alexandria, United Arab Republic.

Public Information Officer, Regional Office of WHO for South-East Asia, Patiala House, Princes Park, New Delhi, India.

Public Information Officer, Regional Office of WHO for the Western Pacific, Post Box 2932, Manila, Philippines.

Public Information Officer, WHO Regional Office for Africa, P.O. Box 6, Brazzaville, Congo (Brazzaville).

International Bank for Reconstruction and Development. International Bank for Reconstruction and Development, 1818 H Street, N.W., Washington 25, D.C., U.S.A.

4, avenue d'Iéna, Paris-16e, France.

International Finance Corporation. International Finance Corporation, 1818 H Street, N.W., Washington 25, D.C., U.S.A.

International Monetary Fund. Office of Public Relations, International Monetary Fund, 19th and H Streets, N.W., Washington 25, D.C., U.S.A.

4, avenue d'Iéna, Paris-16e, France.

International Civil Aviation Organization. Public Information Section, International Civil Aviation Organization, Room 828, International Aviation Building, 1080 University Street, Montreal 2, Quebec, Canada.

European and Africa Office, 60*bis*, avenue d'Iéna, Paris-16e, France.

Far East and Pacific Office, Sala Santithan, Rajadamnoen Avenue, Bangkok, Thailand.

Middle East Office, 16 Hassau Sabri, Zamalek, Cairo, U.A.R.

North American and Caribbean Office, 540 Avenida Chapultepec, 7th floor, México D.F., Mexico.

Universal Postal Union. Universal Postal Union, Case Postale, Berne 15, Switzerland.

International Telecommunications Union. International Telecommunications Union, Place des Nations, Geneva, Switzerland.

World Meteorological Organization. World Meteorological Organization, 41 Avenue Giuseppe Motta, Geneva, Switzerland.

1, quai Branly, Paris-7^e, France.

International Trade Organization. Information and Library Unit, Interim Commission for the International Trade Organization, Villa le Bocage, Geneva 10, Switzerland.

Inter-Governmental Maritime Consultative Organization. Chancery House, Chancery Lane, London, W.C.2, United Kingdom.

National United Nations Associations affiliated with the World Federation of United Nations Associations (WFUNA)

Regular Members of the Federation

Argentina. Asociación Argentina pro Naciones Unidas ' Ana M. Berry ', Paseo Colon 255 P.B. Izq., Buenos Aires.

Australia. United Nations Association of Australia, P.O. Box 48, North Hobart, Tasmania.

Austria. Oesterreichische Liga für die Vereinten Nationen, Boesendorferstrasse 9, Vienna I.

Belgium. Association Belge pour les Nations Unies, Palais d'Egmont, 8 place du Petit Sablon, Brussels 1.

Brazil. Asociacão Brasileira pro Naçoes Unidas, Rua México 41, Rio de Janeiro.

Bulgaria. Association Bulgare pour les Nations Unies, 6, rue Slavianska, Sofia.

Canada. United Nations Association in Canada, 329 Bloor Street W., Toronto 5.

Cuba. Asociación Cubana de las Naciones Unidas, Calle J no. 514, esq. a 25, Havana.

Czechoslovakia. Ceskoslovenska Spolecnost pro Mezinarodni Styky, Loretanska ul. c. 13, Prague I, Hradcany.

Denmark. Den danske FN-forening, 60 St. Kongensgade, Copenhagen K.

Dominican Republic. Asociacion Dominicana pro Naciones Unidas, Secretaria de Estado, Santo Domingo.

Finland. Suomen YK-liitto, Finlands FB-förbund r. y. ; Hallituskatu 17 VI., Helsinki.

France. Association Française pour les Nations Unies, 5, rue Louis le Grand, Paris-2e.

Greece. Association Hellénique pour les Nations Unies, 20, rue Asklipiou, Athens.

Hungary. Magyar Ensz Tarsasag, Dorottya utca 8, Budapest B.

Indonesia. Indonesian United Nations Association, Menteng 25, Jakarta.

Iran. Association Iranienne pour les Nations Unies, Teheran.

Israel. Israel Association for the United Nations, P.O. Box 628, Jerusalem.

Italy. Società Italiana per la Organizzazione Internazionale, Palazzetto di Venezia, Via San Marco 3, Rome.

Japan. United Nations Association of Japan, Naka 4th Bldg., 63-chome, Marunouchi, Chiyoda-ku, Tokyo.

Liberia. Liberian United Nations Association, P.O. Box 547, Monrovia.

Luxembourg. Association Luxembourgeoise pour les Nations Unies, 5, rue Notre-Dame, Luxembourg.

Netherlands. V.I.R.O., Molenstraat 15a., The Hague.

New Zealand. United Nations Association of New Zealand, P.O. Box 1011, Wellington.

Norway. Norsk Samband for de Forente Nasjoner, Parkveien 12, Oslo.

Pakistan. Pakistan United Nations Association, 22-C Garden Road, Karachi 3.

Philippines. United Nations Association of the Philippines, Department of Foreign Affairs Building, Padre Faura, Manila.

Poland. Polskie Towarzystwo Przyjaciol ONZ, Warecka I a., Warsaw.

Rumania. Asociatia Romîna Pentru Natiunile Unite, Str. Biserica Amzei Nr. 5-7, Bucharest.

Sierra Leone. United Nations Association, Jolliboy's Chambers, 22 Charlotte Street, Freetown.

Sweden. Svenska FN-Förbundet, Kronobergsgatan 27, Stockholm K.

Switzerland. Association Suisse pour les Nations Unies, Finkenhubelweg 10, Berne.

Thailand. United Nations Association of Thailand, Santitham Hall, Makawan Rangsan Bridge, Amphut Phra Nakorn, Bangkok.

Turkey. Association Turque pour les Nations Unies, Cocuk Esirgeme Kurumu Apartmani, Yenisehir, Ankara.

Union of Soviet Socialist Republics. Association pour l'Organisation des Nations Unies en U.R.S.S., 19 I Tcheremouchkinskaia, Moscow B-36.

United Kingdom. United Nations Association of Great Britain and Northern Ireland, 25 Charles Street, London, W.1.

United States of America. American Association for the United Nations, 345 East 46th Street, New York 17, N.Y.

Yugoslavia. Fédération des Associations yougoslaves pour les Nations Unies, Proleterskih brigada 74, Belgrade.

Associate Members of the Federation

Burma. Burma Council of World Affairs, Director, Central Statistical and Economic Department, P.O. Box 620, Rangoon.

Ceylon. United Nations Association of Ceylon, 'Ayodhya', 14 Flower Terrace, Colombo 7.

Germany. German Association for the United Nations, Simrockstrasse 23, Bonn.

Ghana. United Nations Association of Ghana, P.O. Box 640, Accra.

Hong Kong. United Nations Association of Hong Kong, 2 Wyndham Street, 2nd Floor, Hong Kong.

Iceland. United Nations Association of Iceland, Tjarnargata 16, Reykjavik.

India. Indian Federation of United Nations Associations, 23 Daryaganj, Delhi 6.

Ireland. United Nations Association, Supreme Court of Justice, Four Courts, Dublin.

Korea. United Nations Association of the Republic of Korea, The Building of the Chamber of Commerce, Rm. 106, 111 Sokong-dong, Choong-ku, Seoul.

Malaya. United Nations Association—Federation of Malaya, 1 Lorong Abdullah, Kuala Lumpur.

Nepal. United Nations Association of Nepal, 522 Dilli Bazar, Kathmandu.

Nigeria. United Nations Association of Nigeria, 9 Ogunlana Drive, Itire Estate, Yaba, Lagos.

South Africa (Republic of). United Nations Association of South Africa, 23 5th Avenue, Parktown North, Johannesburg.

Togo. Association des Nations Unies du Togo, Boîte Postale 677, 9, rue d'Amoutivé, Lomé.

United Arab Republic. Arab Association for the United Nations in the U.A.R., 47 Kasr El-Nil Street, Cairo.

Republic of China.[1] United Nations Association of the Republic of China, 15 Chuan Chow Street, Taipei, Taiwan.

Unaffiliated Associations for the United Nations

Cyprus. United Nations Association of Cyprus, 3 Anthemiou Str., Nicosia.

German Democratic Republic. Deutsche Liga für die Vereinten Nationen, Thälmannplatz 8-9, Berlin, W.8.

Jamaica. United Nations Association of Jamaica, c/o Currency Department, Treasury Buildings, Kingston.

Mexico. Comité Mexicano Pro-Naciones Unidas, Paseo de la Reforma 476, México D.F.

Mongolian People's Republic. Permanent Committee, Mongolian United Nations Association, P.O. Box 363, Ulan-Bator.

Unesco Depository Libraries

The following libraries have accepted to act as reference centres for information on Unesco. They normally receive copies of all Unesco publications, periodicals and other information materials and documen-

1. Association whose status remains undetermined.

tation. They will be able to supply or obtain any of these items for reference use at the library. Those marked with an asterisk (*) also receive United Nations materials.

Albania
Bibliothèque Nationale, Tirana.

Argentina
Centro de Documentación Internacional, a/c Intendente de la Facultad de Derecho y Ciencias Sociales, Ava. Figueroa Alcorta 2263, Buenos Aires.

*Universidad Nacional de Córdoba, Obispo Trejo y Sanabria No. 242, Córdoba.

*Biblioteca Argentina 'Dr. Juan Albarez', Córdoba 1550, Municipalidad de Rosario, Rosario.

Biblioteca Central, Universidad Nacional de Tucuman, San Miguel de Tucuman.

Biblioteca Pública, Universidad Nacional de la Plata, La Plata.

Australia
Public Library of South Australia, Adelaide, South Australia.

Public Library of Queensland, Brisbane, Queensland.

*Commonwealth National Library, Canberra, ACT.

Public Library of Tasmania, Hobart, Tasmania.

*State Library of Victoria, Melbourne, Victoria.

The Library Board of Western Australia, James and Museum Streets, Perth, Western Australia.

*Public Library of New South Wales, Sydney, New South Wales.

Austria
*Oesterreichische National-Bibliothek, Josefsplatz 1, Vienna I.

Belgium
*Bibliothèque du Parlement, Place de la Nation, Brussels.

*Bibliothèque Royale de Belgique, Place du Musée, Brussels.

Bibliothèque de l'Université de Gand, Rozier 9, Ghent.

Bibliothèque de l'Université, Louvain.

Bolivia
*Biblioteca Nacional, Sucre.

Brazil
Reitoria da Universidade da Bahia, Servico Central de Informacoes Bibliograficas, Bahia.

Biblioteca Publica do Estado de Pernambuco, Recife (Pernambuco).

*Biblioteca Nacional, Rio de Janeiro.

Biblioteca Publica Municipal, São Paulo.

Bulgaria

Bibliothèque Centrale, Académie des Sciences de Bulgarie, 1, rue '7' Noemvri, Sofia.
Bibliothèque Nationale 'Ivan Vasov', Plovdiv.
Bibliothèque d'État 'Vassil Kolarov', Bd. Tolbuhin 11, Sofia.

Burma

*National Library, Jubilee Hall, Rangoon.

Byelorussian S.S.R.

*Bibliothèque Publique d'État de Biélorussie 'V. I. Lenin', 9, rue Krasnoarmiejskaja, Minsk.

Cambodia

Bibliothèque Nationale du Cambodge, Boîte Postale No.4, Phnom-Penh.

Canada

Bibliothèque Centrale de l'Université de Montreal, Montreal, Quebec.
*McGill University Library, Montreal, Quebec.
*Bibliothèque de l'Université Laval, Quebec.
*University of Toronto Library, Toronto 5, Ontario.
*University of British Columbia Library, Vancouver, B.C.
Reference Department, University of Alberta Library, Edmonton, Alberta.
Provincial Library of Manitoba, Winnipeg, Manitoba.

Ceylon

The Colombo Public Library, Edinburgh Crescent, Colombo.
The University of Ceylon Library, Peradeniya.
Jaffna College Library, Vaddukodai.

Chile

Biblioteca Nacional, Santiago.
Biblioteca Central, Casilla 20-C, Concepción.
Centro de Documentación, Universidad Austral, Casilla 586, Valdivia.

China

*National Library of Peking, Peking 7.
*National Central Library, Taipei, Taiwan (Formosa).

Colombia

Biblioteca General de la Universidad de Antioquia, Medellín.
Biblioteca Pública Piloto de Medellín para Latino-américa, Av. La Playa No. 42-37, Medellín.
*Biblioteca Nacional, Bogotá.
Universidad del Valle, Biblioteca Central, Apartado Nacional 439, Cali.

Costa Rica
*Biblioteca Nacional de Costa Rica, San José.

Cuba
*Biblioteca Nacional, Havana.
Universidad de Oriente, att. Biblioteca, Santiago de Cuba.

Czechoslovakia
The University Library, Bratislava.
The Provincial and University Library, Zemsky dum II, Zerotinovo namesti, Brno.
The University Library, Bezrucova ulice, Olomouc.
*Bibliothèque Nationale et Universitaire, Klementinum 190, Prague.

Denmark
*Statsbiblioteket i Aarhus, Aarhus.
Det. Kgl. Bibliotek, Copenhagen.

Dominican Republic
Biblioteca de la Universidad de Santo Domingo, Santo Domingo.

Ecuador
*Biblioteca Nacional, Quito.
Universidad de Guayaquil, att. Biblioteca, Casilla de Correo 3834, Guayaquil.

El Salvador
*Biblioteca Nacional del Salvador, San Salvador.

Ethiopia
Bibliothèque Nationale, Addis Ababa.

Finland
Parliamentary Library, Eduskuntatalo, Helsinki.

France
Bibliothèque de l'Assemblée Nationale, 2, rue de Bourgogne, Paris-7e.
Bibliothèque Municipale de Bordeaux, 3, rue Mably, Bordeaux (Gironde).
Bibliothèque de l'Université, place Georges Lyon, Lille (Nord).
Bibliothèque Municipale de Lyon, 4, rue Adolphe Max, Lyon (Rhône).
Bibliothèque Municipale de Marseille, 2, place Auguste Carli, Marseille (Bouches-du-Rhône).
*Bibliothèque Nationale, Service des Publications Officielles, 58, rue de Richelieu, Paris-2e.
Bibliothèque Nationale et Universitaire, 6, place de la République, Strasbourg (Bas-Rhin).
Bibliothèque Municipale, Toulouse (Haute-Garonne).

Federal Republic of Germany

Amerika-Gedenkbibliotek, Am Blücherplatz, Berlin S.W.61.

Bibliothek der Universität, Dundeshaus, Bonn.

Deutscher Bundestag, Bibliothek und Archiv, Bonn.

Stadt- und Universitätsbibliothek, Untermainkai 14-15, Frankfurt-am-Main.

Staats- und Universitätsbibliothek, Moorweidenstrasse 40, 24a, Hamburg 13.

*Max-Planck Institut für Ausländisches, Offentliches Recht und Völkerrecht, Heidelberg.

Bibliothek der Universität, Marburg.

*Staatsbibliothek, Munich.

German Democratic Republic

*Deutsche Staatsbibliothek, Unter den Linden 8, Berlin N.W.8.

Deutsche Bücherei, Deutscher Platz, Leipzig C.1.

Ghana

University College of Ghana, att. The Librarian, P.O. Box 24, Legon, Accra.

Greece

*Bibliothèque Nationale de Grèce, Athènes.

Guatemala

*Biblioteca Nacional, Guatemala.

Haiti

*Bibliothèque Nationale, Port-au-Prince.

Honduras

Biblioteca Nacional, Tegucigalpa.

Hong Kong

The Library, The University, Hong Kong.

Hungary

*Orszaggyulesi Konyvtar, Bibliothèque de l'Assemblée Nationale, Kossuth Lajos tér, Budapest V.

National Szechenyi Library, Muzeum Korut, 14-16, Budapest VIII.

Iceland

*Landsbokasahn Islands, Reykjavik.

India

*Benares Hindu University Library, Benares.

The University Library, Bombay 1.

*The National Library, Belvedere, Calcutta 27.

Delhi Public Library, Queens Road, Delhi 6.

The University Library, Delhi.

State Central Library, Hyderabad, Deccan.
University Library, Lucknow.
*Connemaera Public Library, Madras.
University Library Nagpur, Nagpur, Madhya Pradesh.
*Parliament Library, New Delhi.
Servants of India Society's Library, Poona 4.
The University Library, Travancore, Osmania.

Indonesia
The University Library, Gadjah Mada Univ., Jogjakarta, Central Java.
Libraries Bureau, Djalan Tjilatjap 4, Jakarta.

Iran
Bibliothèque Nationale, Teheran.
Bibliothèque Melli, Tabriz.

Iraq
Baghdad University Central Library, Baghdad.

Ireland
*National Library of Ireland, Kildare Street, Dublin.

Israel
The Haifa Municipal Library, Pevsner House, 54 Pevsner Street, Haifa.
*Jewish National and University Library, Jerusalem.
*The Knesseth (Parliament) Library, The Knesseth Post Office, Jerusalem.
The Municipal Library of Tel Aviv, 8 Montefiore Street, Tel Aviv.

Italy
Biblioteca Universitaria, Cagliari.
*Biblioteca Nazionale, Florence.
Biblioteca Nazionale Braidense, Milan.
Biblioteca Ambrosiana, Prefetto dell'Ambrosiana, 2 piazza Pio XI, Milan.
Biblioteca Nazionale, Naples.
Biblioteca Nazionale, Palermo.
Biblioteca Nazionale Centrale Vittorio Emanuele II, 27, via del Collegio Romano, 27, Rome.
Biblioteca Nazionale, 19, via Po, Turin.

Japan
Aichi Library of the Aichi Cultural Centre, 8 Hisayacho-8-chome, Hugashi-ku, Nagoya-Shi, Aichi-Ken.
University of the Ryukyus, att. The Library, Naha, Okinawa.
Fukuoka Prefectural Library, Higashi Park, Fukuoka City, Fukuoka.
Kyoto Municipal Library, c/o Kansai-Haiden Building, Karasuma-nishi, Shiokojidori, Shimokyo-ku, Kyoto.

Osaka Prefectural Library, 1-chome, Nakanoshima, Kitaku, Osaka City, Osaka.

Sendai Unesco House Library, 21 Motoara-machi, Sendai.

*National Diet Library, No. 14 1-chome, Nagata-cho, Chiyoda-ku, Tokyo.

Korea

Korea University Library, 1 An-Am-Dong, Seoul.

Lebanon

*Bibliothèque Nationale, Beirut.

Liberia

University of Liberia, Monrovia.

Luxembourg

*Bibliothèque Nationale, Boulevard Royal 14a, Luxembourg.

Malagasy Republic

Bibliothèque Universitaire, B.P. 566, Tananarive.

Malaya (Federation of)

Sarawak Museum and Library, Kuching, Sarawak, Borneo.

University of Malaya, Singapore.

Mauritius

The Mauritius Institute, P.O Box 54, Port Louis.

Mexico

Biblioteca Pública del Estado de Jalisco, Hidalgo 258, Guadalajara.

Biblioteca Nacional de México, Avenida Uruguay 67, México.

Biblioteca Lafragua, Universidad de Puebla, Puebla.

Nepal

Central Library Lal Darbar, Kathmandu.

Netherlands

*Koninklijke Bibliothek, The Hague.

University Library, Leyden.

New Zealand

National Library Service, Private Bag, Wellington, C.1.

General Assembly Library, Parliament House, Wellington, C.1.

Nicaragua

*Biblioteca Nacional, Managua.

Nigeria

Eastern Region Library Board, Private Mail Bag, Enugu.

University College (Library), att. The Librarian, Ibadan.

Norway

The University Library, Bergen.

Universitatsbiblioteket, Oslo.
*The Library of the Royal Norwegian Society of Sciences, Trondheim.

Pakistan
*Liaquat National Library, Karachi.
East Pakistan Central Public Library, Shahbagh, Dacca.

Panama
*Biblioteca Nacional, Panama.

Paraguay
*Biblioteca Nacional, Asunción.

Peru
*Biblioteca de la Universidad de Arequipa, Arequipa.
*Biblioteca Nacional, Lima.

Philippines
Bureau of Public Libraries, att. The Library, Department of Education, Manila.

Poland
*Biblioteca Narodowa, Zaklad Uzupelniania Zbiorow, ul. Hankiewicsa 1, Warsaw 22.
Biblioteca Glowna, Uniwersytet A. Mickiewicz, ul. Ratajczaka 38/40, Poznan.
Biblioteca Jagiellonska, Aleja Mickiewicza 22, Warsaw.
Kancelaria Rady Panstwa, Biblioteca Sejmowa, ul. Wiejska 4, Warsaw.
Biblioteca Zakladu Narodowego, im. Ossolinskich, ul. Szewska 37, Wroclaw.

Porto Rico
Caribbean Organization, 452 Avenida Ponce de Leon, Hato Rey.

Portugal
*Biblioteca Nacional, Lisboa.

Rumania
Biblioteca Centrala de Stat, Serviciul de Schimb cu Strainatatea, Str. Ion Ghica No. 4, Bucarest I.
Bibliothèque Centrale Universitaire de Cluj, Str. Miko No. 2, Cluj.
Bibliothèque Centrale Universitaire de Iassy, Str. Pacurari No. 4, Iassy.

Senegal
Bibliothèque de l'Université de Dakar, Dakar.

Somalia
L'Istituto Superiore di Diritto ed Economica, Mogadiscio.

Spain
Ministerio de Educación Nacional, Secretaría General Técnica, Sección de Estudios y Documentación, Madrid.

Oficina de Educación Iberoamericana (OEI), Instituto de Cultura Hispánica, Avenida de los Reyes Católicos, Ciudad Universitaria, Madrid.
*Biblioteca Nacional, Av. de Calvo Sotelo 20, Madrid.
Biblioteca Central de la Deputación, Carmen 47, Barcelona.
Biblioteca Provincial, Sevilla.

Sudan
The Gordon Memorial College Library, Khartoum.

Sweden
Göteborgs Universitetsbiblioteket, Göteborg 5.
*University Library, Lund.
*Kunglija Biblioteket, Stockholm.
Uppsala University Library, Uppsala.
*Riksdagsbiblioteket, Stockholm.

Switzerland
Bibliothèque Universitaire de Bâle, Schoenbeinstrasse 20, Basle.
Bibliothèque Nationale Suisse, Hallwylstrasse 15, Berne.
Zentralbibliothek, Zürich.

Syrian Arab Republic
Bibliothèque El-Sahirié, Damascus.

Thailand
The National Library, Bangkok.

Turkey
Bibliothèque Nationale, Ankara.
*Université Kutuphanesi, Istanbul.

Uganda
*Makerere College Library, P.O. Box 262, Kampala.

Ukrainian S.S.R.
Bibliothèque Publique d'Etat de l'Académie des Sciences d'Ukraine, 58a, rue Wladimirskaja, Kiev.

Union of South Africa
*South African Public Library, Cape Town.
Natal University Library, P.O Box 1525, Durban.
University of Witwatersrand, att. The Library, 44-781, Milner Park, Johannesburg, Transvaal.
*State Library, P.O. Box 397, Pretoria.

Union of Soviet Socialist Republics
Bibliothèque Publique d'Etat 'M. E. Saltykov-Schtchedrin', 18 rue Sadowaja, Leningrad.
Bibliothèque de l'Académie des Sciences de l'U.R.S.S., Wasilewskij-ostrow, 1 Birzewaja Linja, Leningrad.

Bibliothèque d'Etat de l'U.R.S.S. des Littératures Etrangères, 12 rue Razin, Moscow.
Bibliothèque Scientifique de l'Université de Moscou, Département de Littérature Etrangère, Mokhovaia ul. 9, Moscow K. 9.
Bibliothèque d'Etat de l'U.R.S.S. 'V. I. Lenin', 3 rue Kalinin, Moscow.
*Bibliothèque Fondamentale des Sciences Sociales de l'Académie des Sciences de l'U.R.S.S., 11 rue Frounze, Moscow.

United Arab Republic
*The National Library, Ahmed Maher Square, Cairo.

United Kingdom
*National Library of Wales, Aberystwyth.
*City of Belfast Public Libraries, 15 North Howard Street, Belfast.
Birmingham Public Library, Ratcliffe Place, Birmingham.
*Cambridge University Library, Cambridge.
Edinburgh Public Library, George IV Bridge, Edinburgh.
*The Mitchell Library, North Street, Glasgow C.3.
Central Library, Leeds.
*Public Library, Liverpool.
*British Museum, London.
National Central Library, London.
*Manchester Public Libraries (Central Library), Manchester 2.
*Oxford University Library (The Bodleian Library), Oxford.

United States of America
*University of Texas Library, Austin, Tex.
*Louisiana State University Library, Baton Rouge 3, La.
Gen. Library, University of California, Berkeley 4, Calif.
*Harvard University Library, Cambridge 38, Mass.
*University of North Carolina Library, Chapel Hill, N.C.
*University of Chicago Library, Chicago 37, Ill.
*Cleveland Public Library, 325 Superior Avenue, Cleveland 14, Ohio.
*University Library, University of California, 405 Hilgard Avenue, Los Angeles 24, Calif.
*New York Public Library, Grand Central Station, P.O. Box 1932, New York 17, N.Y.
*St. Louis Public Library, St. Louis, Miss.
*Library of Congress, att. Jennings Wood Esq., Exchange and Gift Division, Washington 25, D.C.
Columbus Memorial Library, Pan American Union, 19th & Constitution, Washington 6, D.C.

Government Documents Collections, Gregg M. Sinclair Library, Honolulu, Hawaii.
University of Hawaii Library, Honolulu.

Uruguay
*Biblioteca Nacional, Montevideo.

Venezuela
*Biblioteca Central, Universidad Central de Venezuela, Caracas.

Viet-Nam
*Ecole Française d'Extrême-Orient, Musée Blanchard de la Brosse, Saigon.

West Indies
*University College of the West Indies, att. The Library, Mona, Jamaica.
University of the West Indies, att. The Library, St. Augustine, Trinidad.

Yugoslavia
*Univerzitetska Biblioteka, 'Svetozar Markovic', Bulevar Revolucije 71, Belgrade.
Bibliothèque Nationale et Universitaire de Ljubljana, Ljubljana.
Sveuičlišna Knjižnica, University Library, Zagreb.